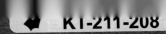

THE WINCHESTER PSALTER

BY FRANCIS WORMALD

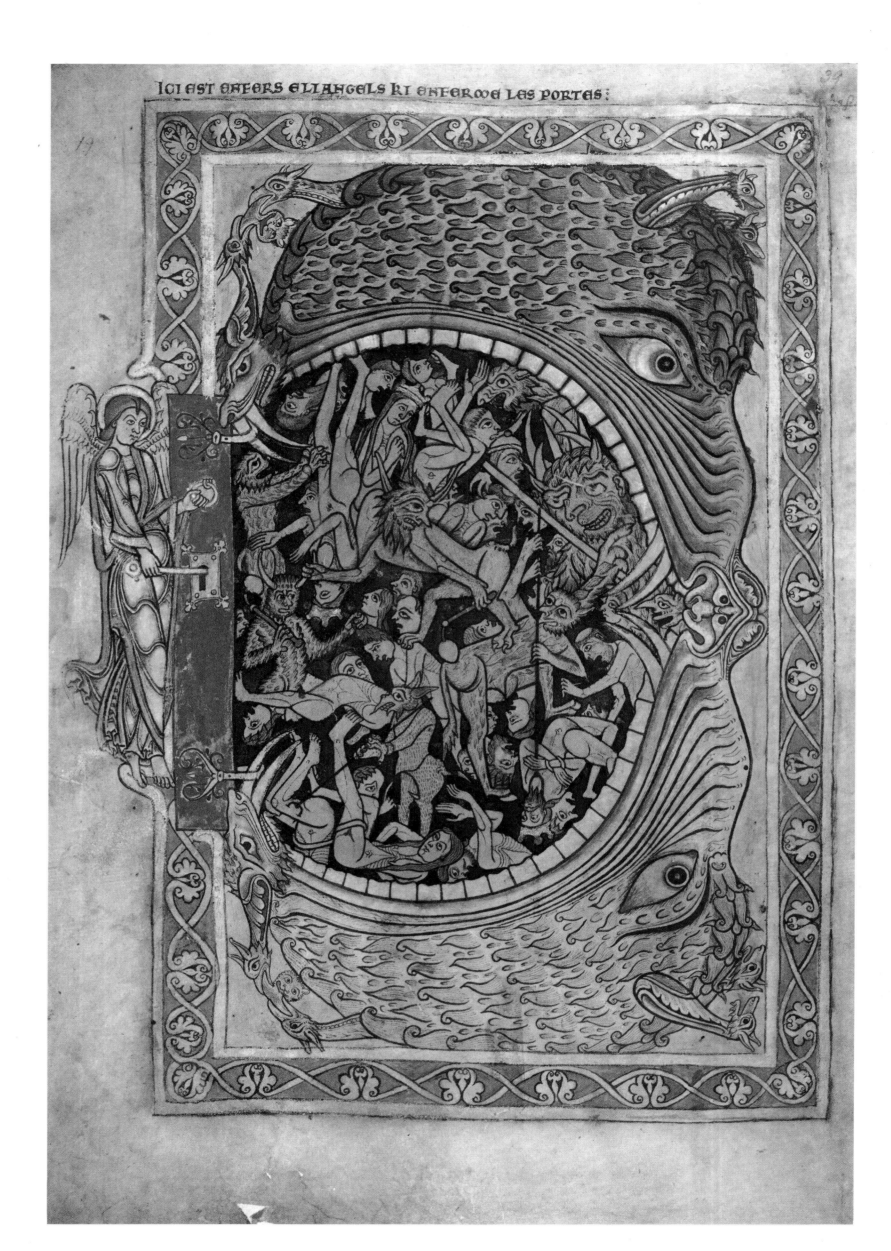

Francis Wormald

THE WINCHESTER PSALTER

with 134 Illustrations

HARVEY MILLER & MEDCALF

© 1973 Harvey Miller & Medcalf Ltd

56 Doughty Street · London WC1N 2LS · England

SBN   85602 008 7

Designed by Elly Miller

Printed at The Curwen Press · Plaistow · London · England

Contents

1. Detail of folio 9 (enlarged)

Preface

When Francis Wormald died on January 11th, 1972 he had completed this book, with the exception of a preface, and he was already awaiting the first proofs from his publisher.

There were a number of books which he had looked forward to writing on his retirement from the Directorship of the Institute of Historical Research and for which he had many ideas and plans. Foremost among these was a History of the 'Winchester School' of Manuscript Illumination, and he was also always fascinated by the British Museum Manuscript Nero C IV—the so-called 'Winchester Psalter' or 'Psalter of Henry of Blois', which is the subject of this book. It was the chance remark of a friend who supposed that he was already working on Nero C IV which made him consider writing about it, even before the 'Winchester School' book, which he had very much in mind; and after some consideration he decided that he would rather enjoy breaking the new ground of Nero C IV first.

In writing this book which is, I believe, the first one published about this important manuscript, Francis Wormald hoped that further research about it might be stimulated and discussion aroused. Nothing has been altered in his text—it stands exactly as he wrote it and nothing has been added except this short preface. He had already discussed the lay-out and illustrations with his publisher Mrs. Miller, and most of these were already chosen, though she has generously included even more than he hoped for and I believe he would have been delighted with the book. My thanks are due to her for all her hard work and enthusiasm in the preparation for publication, as well as to the British Museum for the photographs of the Manuscript, and Professor Kurt Weitzmann of Princeton University, for making available photographs of the Mount Sinai Icons. I should also like to thank Mr. John Beckwith of the Victoria and Albert Museum, Mr. Julian Brown, Professor of Palaeography in the University of London, and Mr. Derek Turner and Miss Janet Backhouse, Department of Manuscripts in the British Museum, who have read the proofs. I am grateful to them all for giving time and skill so generously to do this work.

HONORIA WORMALD
December 1972

2. Christ appears to Mary Magdalene. Detail of folio 24

British Museum Cotton Ms. Nero C IV

DESCRIPTION

Vellum; 12¾in. × 8⅞in., 32·3cm × 22·5cm. Text space 10½in. × 6in., 26·7cm. × 15·2cm. Text written in two columns measuring 26·7cm × 7cm. each column.

BINDING

Modern.

CONTENTS

1 38 full-page miniatures, folios 2–39.

2 Calendar with illustrations of the Labours of the Months and the Signs of the Zodiac, folios 40–45 verso.

3 Psalter in Latin, Gallican version, with an Old French version in the second column, folios 46–123 verso, see S. Berger, *La Bible Française au Moyen Âge*, Paris, 1884, pp. 15, 20–29, 395.

4 Canticles with Old French versions, viz.

    (i)   Confitebor tibi domine (Isaiah xii), folio 123 verso.

    (ii)   Ego dixi in dimidio dierum . . . . (Isaiah xxxviii. 10), folio 124 verso.

    (iii)   Exultauit cor meum . . . . (I Samuel ii), folio 124 verso.

    (iv)   Cantemus domino gloriose . . . . (Exodus xv), folio 125.

    (v)   Domine audiui auditionem . . . . (Habacuc iii. 2), folio 125 verso.

    (vi)   Audite celi . . . . (Deuteronomy xxxii), folio 126 verso.

    (vii) Benedicite omnia opera . . . . (Daniel iii. 57), folio 128 verso.

    (viii) Te Deum laudamus . . . ., folio 129 recto.

    (ix)   Benedictus dominus deus israel . . . . (Luke i.68), folio 129 verso.

    (x)   Magnificat . . . . (Luke i.46), folio 130 recto.

    (xi)   Nunc dimittis . . . . (Luke ii.29), folio 130 recto.

5 Gloria in excelsis, without the French version, folio 130 recto.

6 Pater Noster, with a French version, folio 130 verso.

7 Apostles Creed, with a French version, folio 130 verso.

8 Quicunque uult, with a French version, folio 130 verso–132 recto.

9 Litany, see pp. 123–124, folios 132 recto–132 verso.

10 Collects, mainly found in the *Missale ad usum Ecclesiae Westmonasteriensis*, ed.
J. Wickham Legg (Henry Bradshaw Society, XII), III. 1309, 1310. viz.:

(i)   Deus cui proprium . . . W.M. 1309, folio 133 verso.

(ii)   Omnipotens sempiterne deus qui facis mirabilia . . . W.M. 1309, folio
133 verso.

(iii)   Pretende domine famulis et famulabus tuis dexteram . . . W.M. 1310,
folio 133 verso.

(iv)   Omnipotens sempiterne deus miserere famulo tuo. N. et dirige eum
secundum tuam clementiam in uiam salutis eterne . . ., folio 133 verso.

(v)   Vre igne sancti spiritus renes nostros . . . W.M. 1310, folio 133 verso.

(vi)   Actiones nostras quesumus domine et aspirando preueni . . . W.M. 1310,
folio 133 verso.

(vii)   Deus a quo sancta desideria . . . W.M. 1310, folio 133 verso.

(viii) Da nobis quesumus domine ut animam famuli tui quam de hoc seculo
migrare iussisti. . . ., folio 133 verso.

(ix)   A domo tua quesumus domine spirituales nequitie repellantur et
aeriarum discedat malignitas tempestatum . . . W.M. 1310, folio 133
verso.

(x)   Adesto domine supplicationibus nostris et uiam famulorum tuorum
. . . W.M. 1310, folio 133 verso.

(xi)   Deus qui iustificas impium et non uis mortem pectatorum maiestatem
tuam suppliciter deprecamur ut famulos et famulas tuas de tua
misericordia . . ., folio 134 recto.

(xii)   Animabus quesumus domine famulorum famularumque tuarum et
omnium fidelium defunctorum oratio proficiat supplicantium . . .
W.M. 1311, folio 134 recto.

(xiii) Absolue domine animas famulorum famularumque tuarum ab omni
uinculo delictorum ut in resurrectionis gloria . . . W.M. 1379, folio 134
recto.

(xiv)   Deus qui es sanctorum tuorum splendor mirabilis atque lapsorum
subleuator inenarrabilis . . . W.M. 1311, folio 134 recto.

11 A series of thirty-six prayers in Latin, some with French versions, folios 134
recto–142 verso, as follows:

(i)   'Omnipotens deus et misericors pater et bone domine miserere
mihi peccatori. Da michi ueniam. . . .' [Oratio ad Deum] Migne
Patrologia Latina, clviii. 876, 877; folio 134 recto.

(ii)   'Suscipere digneris domine deus omnipotens laudes et orationes
quas ego indignus orare desidero pro me peccatore. . . .' A long prayer
in which the phrase 'Aue gaude et letare' is followed by a reference
to incidents in the life of Christ. For a similar but shorter prayer,

found in the Shaftesbury Psalter, B.M. Lansdowne MS 383, folio 166, see A. Wilmart, *Auteurs Spirituels et Textes Dévots du Moyen Âge Latin*, p. 328 n.3; folio 134 recto and verso.

(iii) *Oratio*, 'O piissima domina in manus filii tui et tuas commendo animam meam et corpus meum et omnes sensus meos parentes quoque meos et amicos . . .'; folio 134 verso.

(iv) *Oratio de Sancta Maria*, 'Singularis uirgo Maria non aspicias peccata mea. Iniquitates enim mee supergresse sunt caput meum. sicut onus . . .'; folio 135 recto.

(v) *Alia oratio*, 'Aue maria gratia plena . . . Per benedictum fructum benedicti uentris tui domina sanctissima conserua animam et corpus meum. et pro amore dulcissimi tui nati. te deprecor. . . .'; folio 135 recto.

(vi) *Oratio*, 'O Maria piissima. stella maris clarissima. mater misericordie. et aula pudicitie . . .' in verse, Chevalier, *Repertorium Hymnologicum*, 30647; folio 135 recto and verso.

(vii) *Alia oratio*, 'O beata dei genitrix maria piissima domina mea. spes mea. refugium meum. consolatio mea post deum . . .'; folio 135 verso.

(viii) *Alia oratio*, 'Gloriosa dei genitrix uirgo Maria deprecor te ut exaudias orationem meam. et sis mihi et omnibus amicis meis et parentibus et benefactoribus meis miseratrix et adiutrix . . .'; folio 135 verso.

(ix) *Oratio*, 'O domina misericordissima dei et domini mei genitrix. sancta maria dignare meis indignis petitionibus annuere. quas effundere presumo. . . .'; folio 135 verso–136 recto.

(x) *Alia oratio*, 'Sancta maria piarum piissima que nulli negas ausilium gratie tue esto misericors. . . .'; folio 136 recto.

(xi) *Oratio de Sancto Michaele*, 'Sancte Michael archangele qui ueniti in adiutorium in populo dei. subueni michi aput altissimum iudicem. . . .', see A. Wilmart, *Auteurs Spirituels*, pp. 212–3; folio 136 recto.

(xii) *Oratio de Sancto Swithuno*, 'Sancte Swithune beatissime domine. tu es pacificus et omni beatitudine repletus. tu desiderasti Christum. tu es cum Christo in societate sanctorum. Et ego miser peccator et fragilis peccaui in atriis tuis. in domo tua male uiuendo. ac innumera scelera perpetrando. Adiuua me una cum ceteris sanctis quorum corpora in hac iuxta te requiescunt aula. uel quorum reliquie in hac ecclesia uel in hac ciuitate continentur . . . .'; folio 136 recto.

(xiii) *Oratio*, 'Deus inestimabilis misericordie. deus immense pietatis. deus conditor et reparator humani generis. qui confitentium tibi corda purificas. . . .'; folio 136 recto and verso.

(xiv) *Oratio*, 'Auctor totius beatitudinis deus qui omni mansuetudine te humiliter confitentes exaltas. perpetue queso mihi famulo tuo circunda dextere tue pietatis auxilio. . . .'; folio 136 verso.

(xv)   *Oratio*, 'Domine Ihesu Christe rex uirginum integritatis amator. . . .';
        A. Wilmart, *Precum Libelli Quattuor Aevi Carolini*, Rome, 1940,
        pp. 16(11), 140(5); folio 136 verso.

(xvi)   *Oratio*, 'Mane cum surrexero intende ad me domine et guberna
        omnes actus meos. . . .' A version of the 'Oratio sancti Hieronimi
        presbiteri', see A. Wilmart, *Precum Libelli*, p. 10; folio 136 verso–137
        recto.

(xvii) 'Deus o. . . . bone et iuste et anima. . . . medice misericordissime. . . . ego
        confiteor tibi omnia peccata mea que feci in uerbis in factis. in
        cogitatione. . . .'; folio 137 recto.

(xviii) 'Te patrem adoramus eternum. te sempiternum filium inuocamus.
        teque spiritum sanctum in una diuinitatis substantia manentem con-
        fitemur. . . .'; folio 137 recto.

(xix)   'Christe fili dei uiui te suspiro. te esurio. te sicio. te uidere con-
        cupisco. et sicut mater unici filli sui presentia orbata. . . .'; folio 137
        recto–137 verso.

(xx)   *Oratio de Sancto Iohanne baptista*, 'Sancte iohannes baptista qui
        meruisti saluatorem mundi baptizare tuis manibus in fluuio iordanis.
        . . .' *Book of Cerne*, ed. B. Kuypers, p. 156; folio 137 verso.

(xxi)   *Oratio ad Sanctum Petrum*, 'Sancte Petre apostole electe dei. tu con-
        fessus es Christum filium dei uiui. super te edificauit dominus
        ecclesiam suam. . . .'; folio 137 verso.

(xxii) *Oratio ad Sanctum Paulum*, 'Sancte Paule apostole electe dei tu es uas
        electionis. . . .'; folio 137 verso.

(xxiii) *Oratio ad Sanctum Andream*, 'O andrea sancte intercede pro me
        ut euadam pure flammas dure pene. . . .' A shortened form of a
        prayer found in the eleventh century Portiforium of St Wulfstan, see
        edition by A. Hughes (Henry Bradshaw Society XC, 1960, p. 10);
        folio 137 verso.

(xxiv) *Oratio ad Sanctam Iohannem apostolum*, 'Sancte iohannes apostole electe
        dei. te dilexit dominus. . . .', folio 137 verso.

(xxv)   'Omnipotens et misericors deus illumina queso cor meum splendore
        gratie tue. . .'; folio 137 verso.

(xxvi) *Ad Sanctum Katerinam*, 'Deus qui beatissimam uirginem katerinam
        regali stemate oriundam tue cognitionis gratia illustrasti. . . .' A very
        long devotion which recites many of the incidents of the saint's life;
        folio 138 recto and verso.

(xxvii) *Oratio Sancte Fidis uirginis*, 'Sancta et benedicta fides uirgo pretiosa.
        martyr gloriosa. honor celi. decus paradysi. celestis ierusalem mar-
        garita. sponsa Christi. dulcis ac dilecta. . . .'; folio 138 verso.

(xxviii) *Quicumque cantauerit . . . . nem .xii. uicibus valet. . . . psalteria .c. missas .c.
        . . . . .c. oblationes. Et quicumque . . . .cantauerit una vice ualet. . . . .vii.
        psalteria. vii. missas .vii. . . . . tiones .vii. oblationes . . . . altare cantauerit
        multum. . . . aput deum*. et animam eius. . ., 'Deus omnipotens pater

et filius et spiritus sanctus. Trinitas sancta. spes unica. et inestimabilis in tribus personis unitas. Sanctus deus. qui es et qui eras. et qui uenturus es. et idem ipse es. Libera me domine ab. . . .' A version of the Lorica of St Brendan, for other instances of which see A. Wilmart, The Prayers of the Bury Psalter, *Downside Review*, October 1930, p. 16.

(xxix) *Oratio de Sancta Cruce*, 'Domine Ihesu Christe adoro te in cruce ascendentem. . . .' A. Wilmart, Prières Mediévales pour l'Adoration de la Croix, *Ephemerides Liturgicae*, 1932, p. 32 [51]; folio 140 recto.

(xxx) *Oratio*, 'Deus qui beato petro ceterisque apostolis tuis sanctum dedisti spiritum. . . .'; folio 140 recto.

(xxxi) *Oratio* 'Sancta Trinitas atque indiuisa unitas. omnipotens eterne deus. spes unica mundi. . . .', *Book of Cerne*, p. 134; folio 140 recto and verso.

(xxxii) *Oratio de Sancta Maria*, 'Sancta dei genitrix semper uirgo beata benedicta. gloriosa et generosa. intacta et intemerata. . . .' *Book of Cerne*, p. 54; folio 140 verso.

(xxxiii) *Incipit quesitio sancti Augustini. In quacumque die eam cantaueris. neque diabolus neque malus homo nocere ti poterit. Quicquid iustum petieris a domino dabit ti. et si anima tua de corpore egredietur. in inferna non recipietur.* 'Domine Ihesu Christe qui in hunc mundum propter nos peccatores de sinu patris aduenisti. . . .' see A. Wilmart, The Prayers of the Bury Psalter, *Downside Review*, October 1930, p. 5; folios 140 verso–141 verso.

(xxxiv) *Oratio ad petendas lacrimas*, 'Omnipotens mitissime deus qui sitienti populo fontem uiuentis. . . .' Migne, P.L., ci. 117; folio 142 recto.

(xxxv) *Oratio*, 'Omnium sanctorum tuorum intercessionibus quesumus domine gratia tua nos protegat. . . .', with a French version. Found in the eleventh-century English Psalter in Cambridge University Library MS Ff.1.23, folio 281; also in B.M. Arundel MS 155, folio 171 from Christ Church Canterbury; folio 142 recto.

(xxxvi) *Oratio Post Psalterium*, 'Omnipotens et misericors deus clementiam tuam suppliciter deprecor', with a French version . . ., see V. Leroquais, *Les Psautiers Manuscrits latins des Bibliothèques publiques de France*, I, p. ix n.10; folio 142 recto.

(xxxvii) *Oratio*, 'Liberator animarum mundi redemptor ihesu christe domine deus eterne. . . .', with a French version. Found in B.M. Arundel MS 155, folio 191 verso; folio 142 recto.

12 On folio 142 verso at the bottom of the page is an incomplete rubric:

'Incipit liber rationatitorius romano sermone conscriptus de gemina arbore de bono et malo. de uirtutibus et uiciis inter se discordantibus. De die iudicii. de contemptu mundi. De peno dampnationis.' The remainder is lost.

13

Description of the Miniatures

The folio numbers in square brackets refer to the earlier sets of foliation of the miniatures, see p. 69.

FOLIO 2 [folio 1 recto] SCENES FROM THE OLD TESTAMENT
Arranged in three registers.

1   God in the Garden of Eden and the Expulsion from Eden. On the left the Almighty holding in his right hand a scroll inscribed: 'Videte ne forte sumat de ligno uite', cf. Genesis 3.22. With his left hand he points to the Tree of Life. On the right an angel, holding a flaming sword in his right hand, takes Adam by the shoulder as if to press him and Eve who is on the right out of the garden. Both Adam and Eve hold large leaves over their persons.

2   Adam and Eve receive the instruments of work, and work. On the left Adam stands in a furred garment and receives a spade from an angel. Eve in a long robe is given a distaff. On the right Adam delves and Eve spins. The giving of the instruments of work by the angel is found in the thirteenth-century Carrow Psalter in the Walters Art Gallery, Baltimore, see folio 22 verso reproduced in *Illustrations from One Hundred Manuscripts in the Library of Henry Yates Thompson*, IV, London 1914, pl. xx. An angel presents Adam with a hoe in Paris, Bibl. Nat. gr. 510, folio 52 verso, a manuscript of the ninth century, see H. Omont, *Miniatures des plus anciens manuscrits grecs de la Bibliothèque Nationale des VIe au XIVe siècle*, Paris 1929, pl. xxiv.

3   The Story of Cain and Abel (Genesis 4.1–15).
On the left is Abel, a youth, who holds up a lamb towards the Almighty whose head and shoulders are seen emerging from a cloud. To the right is the tall figure of Cain who holds a conventional corn-sheaf. He wears a curious belt with a roundel at the back which has been identified as a 'Belt of Strength' and is worn by the wicked, see G. Zarnecki, A Romanesque Bronze Candlestick in Oslo and the Problem of 'Belts of Strength', Oslo Kunstindustrimuseet, Årbok (1963–64), pp. 45–66. On the right Cain kills Abel with a jaw bone which has become much conventionalised, see G. Henderson, Cain's Jaw-Bone, *Journal of the Warburg and Courtauld Institutes*, XXIV (1961), pp. 108–114.

FOLIO 3 [folio 1 verso] SCENES FROM THE OLD TESTAMENT:
NOAH'S ARK AND THE SACRIFICE OF ISAAC

1   Noah commanded by the Almighty to build the ark (Genesis 6.14).
    On the left the Almighty addresses Noah who has an axe in his right hand
    and with his left holds the prow of the half-finished vessel.

2   The return of the dove to the ark with the olive branch (Genesis 8.11).
    On the left Noah receives the leaf from the dove. The ark is filled with
    humans and animals; the upper storey being occupied by birds. The ark
    tosses upon waves in which are seen the heads of drowned humans and
    animals. On the left a large black bird, the raven of verse 6, pecks at the head
    of a man.

3   The Sacrifice of Isaac (Genesis 22).
    On the left is the Almighty holding a scroll in the left hand. It is inscribed
    'Tolle filium tuum quem diligis Ysaac' (Genesis 22.2). With the right hand
    he points to Abraham. On the right is the scene of sacrifice. Abraham is about
    to kill Isaac who crouches on the top of the altar, but his sword is seized by
    an angel in whose left hand is a scroll inscribed: 'Ne extendas manum tuam
    super puerum' (cf. Genesis 22.12). Rather similar iconography for this last
    scene is in the Lambeth Bible, folio 6, see C. R. Dodwell, *The Great Lambeth
    Bible*, London 1959, pl. 1.

FOLIO 4 [folio 2 recto] SCENES FROM THE OLD TESTAMENT AND
THE APOCRYPHAL GOSPELS
In three registers.

1   Moses and the Burning Bush (Exodus 3.2–4), and Moses receiving the Tables
    of the Law on Mount Sinai (Exodus 31.18).
    On the left stands Moses holding a long staff, cf. Exodus 4.2, 3. In front of him
    is a tree at the foot of which is a flaming circle in which is a figure of a beard-
    less man who addresses Moses. This is the flame of the burning bush which is
    not burnt up, see Exodus 4.3.
    On the right Moses receives the Tables of the Law from the hand of God
    which emerges from a cloud.

2   The Almighty with David and Solomon(?).
    It is not clear what this scene represents. Apparently it shows the Almighty
    presenting a sceptre to the king on the left and a book to the king on the
    right. It is conceivable that David and Solomon are meant. The explanation
    offered by Walter Cahn, The Tympanum of the Portal of Saint-Anne,
    Journal of the Warburg and Courtauld Institutes, XXXII (1969), p. 64, seems far-
    fetched.

3   Angel appearing to Joachim.
    On the left is an angel with a scroll inscribed: 'Noli timere ioachim ego . . .
    angelus domini'. In the middle Joachim, a young man, stands in front of his

flocks. The story comes from the apocryphal Infancy Gospels, see M. R. James, *The Apocryphal New Testament*, Oxford 1924, pp. 38–49, 79–80. It is an early example of this scene. The rest of the story of the birth of the Virgin is on folio 8.

FOLIO 5 [folio 2 verso] SCENES FROM THE OLD TESTAMENT: STORIES OF JACOB AND JOSEPH

Arranged in three registers.

1a Jacob wrestling with the angel (Genesis 32.22–32). The angel holds a scroll inscribed: 'Dimitte me quia iam aurora est', cf. Genesis 32.26. Jacob's scroll reads: 'Non dimittam te nisi benedixeris mihi', Genesis 32.27.

b Jacob's dream of the ladder (Genesis 28.10–14).
Jacob with his head on a large rectangular stone, see verse 11. From behind him a ladder stretches up to heaven. A bust of the Almighty appears from a cloud above.

2a Joseph and Potiphar's wife (Genesis 39.12). On the left Joseph turns and admonishes Potiphar's wife who is seated on a couch and tugs with her right hand at Joseph's cloak.

b Potiphar's wife accuses Joseph to her husband who is represented as a king, by showing him Joseph's cloak (Genesis 39.16).

3a Joseph shut in a tower. It is not clear whether this shows Joseph's imprisonment (Genesis 39.20) or Joseph being summoned to interpret Pharaoh's dream (Genesis 41.14).

b Joseph preferred by Pharaoh (Genesis 41.40). Pharaoh who is crowned presents Joseph with a sceptre.

FOLIO 6 [folio 3 recto] SCENES FROM THE LIFE OF DAVID

Four scenes in two registers.

1a David before Saul rejects Saul's armour (1 Samuel 17.39).
Saul crowned and seated holds out a coat of mail towards David standing before him. He holds up his sling and staff, cf. 1 Samuel 17.49. Behind Saul there are a number of courtiers.

b David and Goliath.
On the right David strikes Goliath on the forehead with a stone from his sling (1 Samuel 17.49). Actually David has a stone in his sling. What is shown is really two actions: The first is the actual act of slinging and secondly the result to Goliath. Behind David is a group of Israelites.

2a David beheads Goliath.
This scene is on the right of the composition. David bends over the giant. Behind him the Philistines retreat, see 1 Samuel 51.32.

b David brings the head of Goliath to Saul.
On the right a youthful David holds up the head of the giant to Saul. Behind are courtiers and soldiers, cf. 1 Samuel 17.57, 58.

FOLIO 7 [folio 3 verso] SCENES FROM THE LIFE OF DAVID

1   David as a shepherd rescuing a sheep from the lion (1 Samuel 17.34–36).
    Inscription: ICI ESCVST DAVID AL LIVN VN VEILLE.
    On the left stands David holding a crook. Before him gambol two goats. In
    the middle is a large tree with conventional foliage. On the right is a lion with
    a lamb in its mouth. A youthful David takes hold of the lamb.

2   Anointing of David by Samuel (1 Samuel 16.13).
    Inscription: ICI ENVNIST SAMVEL LI PRHETE DAVID EN REI PAR LV
    CVMADT DEV.
    On the right stands Samuel with his left hand raised. In his right hand he
    holds the horn of oil which he pours over David's head. David is shown as a
    boy. In the middle stands Jesse. Behind him are David's six brothers.

FOLIO 8 [folio 4 recto, VI recto] SCENES FROM THE LIFE
OF THE BLESSED VIRGIN

1a Annunciation of the impending birth of the Virgin to St Anne.
    The angel holds a scroll and addresses St Anne who is standing, cf. Protevan-
    gelium IV.1, M. R. James, *The Apocryphal New Testament*, Oxford 1924, p. 40.

b   Joachim and Anne, the parents of the Virgin, meet at the Golden Gate of the
    Temple, cf. Protevangelium LV.4, M. R. James, *loc. cit.*
    The gate is a very stylised affair.

2   The Birth of the Virgin.
    This scene apparently shows Anne asking the midwife about her child, see
    Protevangelium V.2, M. R. James, *op. cit.*, p. 41. Anne lies on a bed and
    addresses a woman holding the child.

3   Presentation of the Virgin in the Temple.
    Inscription: ICI OFFRE AL TEMPLE . . . . SECVN LA LEI.
    Anne holds the child over an altar. On the left is Joachim holding up a pair
    of birds. Behind him is a servant with two more birds.
    This is a very early series of pictures of the life of the Virgin which was to
    become a common theme in the thirteenth century. Actually most of the
    iconography of this miniature has been borrowed from pictures of the
    Infancy of Christ. Thus the scene of the angel and St Anne is to all intents and
    purposes an Annunciation, while St Anne and the midwife comes from a
    Nativity combined with a seated Virgin and Child. The Presentation of the
    Virgin is virtually the scene of the Presentation of Christ in the Temple on
    folio 34 verso of the Benedictional of St Aethelwold.

FOLIO 9 [folio 4 verso, VI verso] THE TREE OF JESSE

    There is a fragment of an inscription at the top of the leaf. At the foot of the
    tree Jesse lies asleep. From his body springs the great tree from whose
    branches grows fantastic foliage. On the middle axis is a king, the Blessed
    Virgin crowned, Christ and above the Holy Ghost in the form of a dove. Two
    tall prophets with scrolls stand on either side. They may be intended for

Abraham and Moses, see A. Watson, *The Early Iconography of the Tree of Jesse*, Oxford 1934, p. 104, who suggests a similarity to the Tree of Jesse in the slightly earlier Shaftesbury Psalter, B.M. Lansdowne MS 383, folio 15 recto.

FOLIO 10 [folio 5 recto] SCENES FROM THE LIFE OF CHRIST

1a The angel Gabriel sent to the Virgin Mary.

Inscription: ICI ANVNTIE LI ANGELS A NOSTER DAME NOSTER SALVT.

The Almighty sitting in a mandorla addresses an angel. This scene is based upon Luke 1.26: 'And in the sixth month the angel Gabriel was sent from God unto a city of Galilee, named Nazareth'. A very similar representation is to be found in the Shaftesbury Psalter, B.M. Lansdowne MS 383, folio 12v, see E. G. Millar, *English Illuminated Manuscripts from the Xth to the XIIIth Century*, Paris and Brussels 1926, pl. 33a.

b The Annunciation.

Inscription: ICI ENTRET LI SAINZ ESPIRS EN LI.

The scene takes place under an arched building with turrets. On the left stands the archangel Gabriel holding a palm. The Virgin has risen from her seat and is holding a book. Above her is the Holy Ghost in the form of a dove. The Virgin with a book is discussed in great detail by O. Pächt in *The St. Albans Psalter* (Albani Psalter), London 1960, pp. 63–67, where it is of some interest to note that the Virgin with a book is found at Cluny as well as England.

2a The Visitation (Luke 1.39–55).

Inscription: ICI BAISE SAINTE MARIE ELISABET.

The scene takes place under an arch with curtains on each side. These curtains are found in the eighth-century English ivory of Genoels-Elderen in the Musée du Cinquantenaire in Brussels, see F. Volbach, *Elfenbeinarbeiten der Spätantike und des frühen Mittelalters*, Mainz 1952, pl. 6a.

b The Nativity of Christ.

Inscription: ICI ENFANTET NOSTER DAME IESV CRIST ICI GIST IES CRIST EN LA CRECHE.

Under a round headed arch the Virgin lies on a bed. On the left at the foot sits Joseph. On the right at the head of the bed is the midwife who stretches out her right hand. It is possible though by no means certain, that this refers to the unbelieving Salome of the Gospel of Thomas, see M. R. James, *The Apocryphal New Testament*, Oxford 1924, pp. 46, 47. The iconography of this scene with the Child in the manger in front and the midwife at the head of the bed should be compared with the miniature in the Benedictional of St Aethelwold, folio 15 verso.

FOLIO 11 [folio 5 verso] SCENES FROM THE LIFE OF CHRIST

1 The Annunciation to the Shepherds (Luke 2.8–14).

Inscription: ICI ANVNCENT LI ANGEL AS PASTVRES LA NATIVITE NOSTRE SEIGNVR.

Above are three angels, below are four shepherds. The foremost angel holds a scroll inscribed: 'Natus est nobis hodie saluator,' cf. Luke 2.11, and the angel in the middle holds a scroll inscribed: 'Qui est Christus dominus in ciuitate dauid,' Luke 2.11. The gesture of the young shepherd hiding his head in his hood in awe is already suggested in the miniature of this scene in the St.Albans Psalter, see *The Saint Albans Psalter*, pl. 17a.

2   The Magi before Herod (Matthew 2.7, 8).
Inscription: ICI VIENENT LI TREI REI A HERODE.
On the right sits Herod in the doorway of a building holding a sword in his right hand and in his left hand a scroll inscribed: 'Ite et interrogate diligenter de puero,' Matthew 2.8. On the left are the three kings.

FOLIO 12 [folio 6 recto, VIII recto] SCENES FROM THE LIFE OF CHRIST

1   The Journey of the Magi to Bethlehem (Matthew 2.10).
Inscription: ICI LVRAREIST LESTEILE KIS MEINET EN BETHLEEM.
A thirteenth-century hand has added a similar inscription above this twelfth-century one.
The three kings ride from left to right and the foremost horse is already half out of the picture.

2   The Adoration of the Magi (Matthew 2.11).
Inscription: ICI AORENT NOSTRE SEIGNVR E OFRENT LI OR E ENCENS E MIRRE.
In the right hand margin there is a thirteenth-century inscription: 'Ici aor nostre seignur e li offrent [or] e encens e mirre.' The foremost king offers a ring; the second who is beardless holds a covered box, the third a phial.

FOLIO 13 [folio 6 verso, VIII verso] SCENES FROM THE LIFE OF CHRIST

1   The Magi warned by an angel to flee from Herod (Matthew 2.12).
Inscription: ICI LV APAREIST LI ANGELS SIS RVV ET ALER EN LVR CVNTRE PAR AVTRE VEIE.
On the right an angel addresses the kings; two are sleeping and the third starts up.

2   Joseph warned by an angel to go to Egypt (Matthew 2.13).
Inscription: ICI CVMANDET LI ANGELS A IOSEPH KIL MAINT LEMFANT E LA DAME EN EGYPTE.
Joseph in bed addressed by an angel. In the middle is a lamp. This scene is known in the Echternach Gospels in Nürnberg and also in the eleventh-century Italian Gospels of Matilda of Tuscany in the Pierpont Morgan Library in New York, see G. F. Warner, *Gospels of Matilda, Countess of Tuscany*, Roxburghe Club 1917, pl. xii.

FOLIO 14 [folio 7 recto, IX recto] SCENES FROM THE LIFE OF CHRIST

1   Flight into Egypt (Matthew 2.14).
Inscription: ICI VAIT IOSEPH EN EGYPTE OD LEMFANT E OD LA MERRE.
Joseph on the right turns back towards the Virgin. He has a tool over his

shoulder. The Virgin rides side-saddle. On either side are two towers representing presumably Bethlehem and Egypt. Joseph looking round is also found in the Gospels of Matilda of Tuscany, *ed. cit.*, pl. xii.

2   Massacre of the Innocents (Matthew 2.16).

Inscription: ICI FAIT HERODE OCIRRE LES INNOCENS; written over the arch.

In the right margin the thirteenth-century hand has written: 'Ici feyt herode ocirre l [es] innoce [ns].' On the left Herod accompanied by a man in armour. In the middle another soldier and a grotesque negroid giant murder children. This gigantic figure seems to be a particularly English contribution to the scene. On the right are the mothers of the children, cf. v. 18 'In Rama was there a voice heard, lamentation and great mourning, Rachel weeping for her children and would not be comforted, because they are not'.

FOLIO 15 [folio 7 verso, IX verso] SCENES FROM THE LIFE OF CHRIST

1   Presentation in the Temple (Luke 2.22–34).

Inscription: ICI OFFRET LA DAME LEMFANT A SAINT SIMEON AL TEMPLE.

The aged Simeon takes the Child which is held by the Virgin above an altar. On the left is a servant holding two pairs of birds, cf. Luke 2.24: 'And to offer a sacrifice according to that which is said in the law of the Lord, a pair of turtle doves or two young pigeons.' Joseph is not represented.

2   Christ among the doctors (Luke 2.46, 47).

Inscription: ICI SIET IESVS CHRISTVS EN MI LES MAISTRES DE LA LEI AL TEMPLE.

Under an arcade is the young Christ seated holding a book. On either side are groups of men. The general arrangement of the scene and the solemn pose of Christ recalls the mosaic of this scene at Monreale, see O. Demus, *The Mosaics of Norman Sicily*, London 1949, pl. 65B.

FOLIO 16 [folio 8 recto, X recto] SCENES FROM THE LIFE OF CHRIST

1   Mary and Joseph find Jesus in the Temple (Luke 2.48).

Inscription: ICI LV TRVVAT MARIE E IOSEPH.

In the middle the youthful Christ standing on a cloud. He holds a scroll. Above is the hand of God. Joseph and Mary on both sides. Three of the pillars have carved capitals; a griffin and two animals. This scene is usually combined with the previous one. The hand of God may be a reference to Luke 2.49: 'And he said unto them, How is it that ye sought me? wist ye not that I must be about my Father's business?'

2   Baptism of Christ (Mark 1.9–11).

Inscription: ICI LV BAPTIZAT SAINT IOHANS.

The Baptist is on the left. Christ in the middle on whom descends the dove. On the right is the angel with the robe. Jordan which is piled up round Christ's body is full of fish. The angel with the robe is found in both the St Albans Psalter and in the twelfth-century leaf in British Museum Add. MS 37472(1), verso, see M. R. James, *The Walpole Society*, vol. 25 (1936–37), pl. IV.

3. The Marriage at Cana. Folio 17

FOLIO 17 [folio 8 verso, X verso] SCENES FROM THE LIFE OF CHRIST

1   Marriage at Cana (John 2.1–11).
    Inscription: ICI EVT AS NOCES OD ARCHITRICLIN.
    In the middle sits the master of the feast, Architriclinus. The Virgin is on his
    left and Christ on the left of the Virgin. She turns to Christ to announce the
    lack of wine, cf. v. 3. Drinking vessels are absent from the table except for a
    large horn held by the master of the feast. This scene is found in the English
    twelfth-century miniature in B.M. Add. MS 37472(1) verso, but in an entirely
    different form, see M. R. James, *Walpole Society*, vol. 25, pl. IV.

2   Drawing the water and filling the waterpots for the miracle (John 2.7).
    Inscription: ICI FIST DEL EVE VIN.
    The waterpots are kept in a large cupboard on the left. On the right a youth
    draws water from a well placed under a splendid ornamental tree. Diagon-
    ally across the picture is a staircase leading up to the feast taking place in, as
    it were, an upper storey.

FOLIO 18 [folio 9 recto, XI recto] SCENES FROM THE LIFE OF CHRIST

1   First and Second Temptations of Christ (Matthew 4.1–6).
    Inscription: ICI LO RVVAT DEIABLES KE IL FESIST DE PIERES PAIN AL
    DESERT. ICI LO RVVAT DESCENDRE DEL PINNACLE DEL TEMPLE.
    The two scenes are divided from one another by a tree. On the left the devil
    points to stones at his feet. On the right the devil admonishes Christ who
    stands on a pinnacle.

2   Third Temptation (Matthew 4.8).
    Inscription: written in red in the right margin in a thirteenth-century hand:
    'Ici offert obeyse de tute munde. Ihesus sun seignur commandet ariere.'
    On the right Christ standing on a hill, cf. v. 8, addresses the devil who holds
    out a bracelet. Scattered about are various objects expressive of worldly
    possessions. The devil is winged and wears a fantastic woman's (?) dress with
    long knotted sleeves and skirt. For a discussion of earlier versions of this
    scene see O. Pächt, *The St. Albans Psalter*, p. 86, where the bird beaked devil
    is considered to be particularly English. The devil holds a scroll inscribed
    'Hec omnia tibi dabo si adoraueris me,' cf. Matthew 4.9; Christ has one
    saying: 'Vade retro satane non temptabis dominum deum tuum,' cf. Luke
    4.12.

FOLIO 19 [folio 9 verso, XI verso] SCENES FROM THE LIFE OF CHRIST

1   The Raising of Lazarus (John 11).
    Christ on the left with a group of apostles. He holds a scroll inscribed:
    'Tollite lapidem' (John 11.39). In front lies Mary prostrate, cf. John 11.32.
    Lazarus in grave clothes lies in a rectangular sarcophagus the lid of which is
    raised by a crowd of Jews. The iconography is different from the Chichester
    reliefs and the drawing in Cambridge, Pembroke College MS 120, folio 1
    verso, see E. Parker, A Twelfth-Century Cycle of New Testament Drawings

from Bury St Edmunds Abbey, *Proceedings of the Suffolk Institute of Archaeology*, XXXI (1969), pp. 263–302, especially pp. 274–6.

2   Entry into Jerusalem (Luke 11.6–11).
Christ in the middle rides astride. Behind him is a group of disciples. On the left a youth hacks down branches from a tree. On the right is the city in the gate of which is a group of bearded men. The windows are filled with spectators, many of them beardless. This distinction may owe something to Byzantine iconography. The earlier English examples, e.g. Cotton MS Tiberius C.VI, folio 11, and Pembroke College MS 120, folio 2 verso, where the crowd tends to be beardless, see F. Wormald, An English Eleventh Century Psalter with Pictures, *Walpole Society*, 38, pl. 10, and E. Parker, *op. cit.*, pl. xxxv.

FOLIO 20 [folio 10 recto, XII recto] SCENES FROM THE LIFE OF CHRIST

1   The Last Supper.
Inscription: On the top border, but illegible.
The scene takes place under three arches surmounted by an elaborate congerie of roofs and pinnacles. Christ in the middle with a bearded St John leaning against him. Apostles on either side. Christ holds the Host in his right hand and supports the Chalice with the left. An interesting feature is the way in which St Peter places his right hand over the Host and the apostle on Christ's left takes hold of the Chalice. This clearly refers to the institution of the Eucharist. Judas lies in front of the table. For valuable comments on the iconography of this scene see O. Pächt, *The St. Albans Psalter*, p. 58.

2   Christ washes the feet of the Apostles (John 13.4–20)
Inscription: ICI LAVAT LES PIEZ AS APOSTLES.
The apostles are seated in a bunch on the right. Christ on the left kneels on one knee. St Peter holds up both hands in protest. Behind Christ is a bearded man holding a long towel over his shoulder. This last figure is also found in the twelfth-century drawing in Cambridge, Pembroke College MS 120, folio 3 recto, see E. Parker, *op. cit.*, pl. xxxvi. A similar attendant is in the Psalter of St Louis, Paris Arsenal MS lat 1186, folio 22, see E. Kantorowicz, The Baptism of the Apostles, *Dumbarton Oaks Papers*, 9, 10 (1956), fig. 27.

FOLIO 21 [folio 10 verso, XII verso] SCENES FROM THE LIFE OF CHRIST

1   The Betrayal (Mark 14.43, 44).
Christ in the middle embraced by Judas who is clean shaven. No apostles are to be seen except for St Peter who stands behind Christ and strikes off the ear of Malchus who stands on the right. The crowd is made particularly grotesque and savage. The general arrangement of the scene has certain parallels with Pembroke MS 120, folio 3 recto, though in that manuscript the incident of St Peter and Malchus is placed on the extreme left. Tiberius C.VI, folio 12 has quite a different version.

2 The Flagellation (Matthew 27.26, 27).

Inscription : ICI FVT FLAG . . . EST.

On the left Pilate dressed as a king. A small devil whispers into his ear. The composition is divided by a pillar to which Christ is tethered. The smiters stand on both sides. He on the right is wearing a belt of strength and evil, see G. Zarnecki, A Romanesque Candlestick in Oslo and the Problem of Belts of Strength, Oslo, Årbok, 1963/4, pp. 45–66. The torturers are made particularly savage.

FOLIO 22 [folio 11 recto, XIII recto] SCENES FROM THE LIFE OF CHRIST

1 The Crucifixion.

Christ on the Cross in the centre between two thieves. On his right a soldier pierces his side. On the left a youth holds up the sponge. On either side of the two thieves are men with hammers who break the bones of their legs, cf. John 19.32. On the left stands the Virgin wringing her hands. On the right is St John holding a writing tablet and a stylus. Behind both are crowds of spectators.

In general arrangement the disposition of the figures is similar to Pembroke College MS 120, folio 3 verso, see E. Parker, *op. cit.*, pl. xxxvii, though there the thieves are attached to their crosses by ropes. The figures with hammers are not in the Pembroke manuscript, but are in the twelfth-century English leaves in London, Victoria and Albert Museum MS 661, see M. R. James, *The Walpole Society*, 25 (1936–37), pl. VII. St John with writing materials is found in the late tenth-century English Psalter, B. M. Harley MS 2904, folio 3 verso.

2 The Deposition from the Cross.

In the middle is Christ supported by a bearded man. His right hand has already been loosened and the left hand is still attached to the arm of the cross. Another man is drawing the nail from this hand. On the left the Virgin takes Christ's right hand and kisses it. Another woman stands behind her weeping. The iconography is similar to that in Pembroke MS 120, folio 4, Parker, *op. cit.*, pl. xxxviii, though Pembroke contains more figures and has an extra man who supports Christ's legs. A very similar composition is found on a thirteenth-century icon at St Catharine's, Mount Sinai, see G. and M. Sotiriou, *Icones du Mont Sinaï*, Athens 1956, no. 203.

FOLIO 23 [folio 11 verso, XIII verso] SCENES FROM THE LIFE OF CHRIST

1 The Entombment (John 19.39–42).

Inscription : on the left border IES is visible.

Christ in grave clothes is laid in a sarcophagus by two men. A third man washes the body. Behind are trees, cf. verse 41: 'et in horto monumentum novum in quo nondum quisquam positus erat.' The iconography approximates to the earlier types in which the women and the Virgin are not present.

2 The Women at the Sepulchre (Mark 16.1–5).

Inscription : on the border between the two scenes, illegible.

Three women with censers addressed by an angel sitting on the tomb. Below are three soldiers asleep. In general arrangement this scene is similar to the Benedictional of St Aethelwold, folio 51 verso, except that in the latter as well as the Benedictional of Archbishop Robert and the other Anglo-Saxon representations the angel sits before the entrance to an architectural tomb.

FOLIO 24 [folio 12 recto, XIIII recto] SCENES FROM THE LIFE OF CHRIST

1   The Harrowing of Hell.

Inscription: ICI . . . DESCENTE ENFERS.

Christ holding a cross staff with a banner seizes a figure, Adam, from Hell-mouth which is crowded with naked men and women. Behind him is the archangel Michael with a long staff with which he pierces a devil. Satan lies bound in front. High in the sky on the right the sun is shining.

This scene is found in Cotton MS Tiberius C.VI, folio 14, but is quite differently treated, see F. Wormald, *Walpole Society*, 38, pl. 16. In the St Albans Psalter there are two angels, and Hell is differently represented. Pembroke MS 120, folio 4 verso, see Parker, *op. cit.*, pl. xxxix, is closer though it omits the sun.

2   Christ appears to Mary Magdalene (John 20.15–17).

Inscription: on the upper border, obliterated.

This miniature is composed of two incidents in the story. On the left Mary Magdalene asks Christ where his body is. On the right she recognizes Christ and falls at his feet.

FOLIO 25 [folio 12 verso, XIIII verso] SCENES FROM THE LIFE OF CHRIST

1   St Peter receives the keys (Matthew 16.19).

Inscription: on the upper border, obliterated.

The position of this scene in this place immediately after Christ's appearance to St Mary Magdalene follows the order of St John 20.22, 23; 'And when he had said this, he breathed on them, and saith unto them, Receive ye the Holy Ghost: Whose soever sins ye remit, they are remitted and whose soever sins ye retain, they are retained,' though the reference to the keys appears only in St Matthew.

2   Christ and the disciples on the road to Emmaus (Luke 24.13–28).

Inscription: ICI . . . EN SEMBLANCE DE PELERIN.

On the left Christ as a pilgrim holding a long pilgrim's staff. He addresses the two pilgrims, one of them carrying a long staff. For a discussion of the iconography of this scene see O. Pächt, *The St. Albans Psalter*, pp. 73–79.

FOLIO 26 [folio 13 recto, XV recto] SCENES FROM THE LIFE OF CHRIST

1   The Supper at Emmaus (Luke 24.30).

Inscription: on the upper border, obliterated.

Christ is seated at the table blessing the bread which he holds in his left hand. The disciple on the left who is pouring from a jug starts back in a gesture of recognition. The scene represents the moment of recognition. In general the arrangement is that found at Monreale, see O. Demus, *The Mosaics of Norman Sicily*, London 1950, pl. 73a. The attitude of pouring appears to be a rare feature. In Carolingian and Ottonian representations Christ has already divided the bread, see also Pembroke College MS 120, folio 4 verso, E. Parker, *op. cit.*, pl. xxxix.

2   Christ appears to the Apostles and St Thomas touches the wound in the side of Christ (Luke 24.36 and John 20.26, 27).
Inscription: ICI APARVT AS APOSTLES ET THOMAS LV MANIAT. In the right hand margin the thirteenth-century hand has written, 'Ici aparust as apostles e thomas lu maniat'.
This scene is a conflation of two separate incidents; the first, described by St Luke, is Christ's appearance to the apostles; the second is the incident of doubting Thomas. The same combination is found in the St Albans Psalter, see O. Pächt, *The St. Albans Psalter*, p. 78, also Pembroke MS 120, folio 4 verso, E. Parker, *op. cit.*, pl. xxxix.

FOLIO 27 [folio 13 verso, XV verso] SCENES FROM THE LIFE OF CHRIST

Ascension (Acts 1.9–11).
Inscription: ICI LES GARDAT NOSTRE DAME E LI APOSTLES.
The scene is divided into two registers. In the upper half the lower part of Christ's body disappears into a cloud, verse 9: 'and a cloud received him out of their sight'. The mandorla surrounding Christ is supported by two angels who address the apostles in the lower part of the picture. In the middle is the Virgin with St Peter on the right. This type of Ascension picture has been discussed by M. Schapiro, The Image of the Disappearing Christ, *Gazette des Beaux Arts*, March 1943, pp. 135–152. A very similar Anglo-Saxon representation is found in B.M. Cotton MS Caligula A XIV, folio 18, see Schapiro, *op. cit.*, fig. 6.

FOLIO 28 [folio 14 recto, XVI recto] SCENES FROM THE LIFE OF CHRIST

1   The Descent of the Holy Spirit at Pentecost (Acts 2.1–11).
Inscription: ICI DESCENDIT LI SAINT ESPIRZ SVR LES APOSTLES.
Under a multi-turreted building are the apostles. St Peter is in the middle. Above is the Holy Ghost in the form of a bird from whose beak stream tongues of flame, see verse 3. The iconography seems to follow the Anglo-Saxon practice of omitting the Virgin from the scene. She is found in the St Albans Psalter and in Pembroke College MS 120.

2   Christ in Majesty.
Inscription: ICI DEVS EN SA MAGESTE.
In the right hand margin the thirteenth-century hand has written: 'Ici feit deus en sa maieste.' Christ seated between the Four Beasts. He holds a closed book. The arrangement of the evangelist symbols is:

1 Angel	4 Eagle
2 Calf	3 Lion

FOLIO 29 [folio 14 verso, XVI verso] THE BYZANTINE DIPTYCH

The Death of the Virgin.

Inscription: ICI EST LA SVMTION DE NOSTRE DAME. In the right margin a twelfth-century hand has written 'deus'.

As has been pointed out many times the iconography of this miniature follows very closely that of the Byzantine Koimesis, see F. Saxl and R. Wittkower, *British Art and the Mediterranean*, Oxford 1948, 24.6, 7. The Hand of God above is unusual, though the door of Heaven is sometimes shown opening.

FOLIO 30 [folio 15 recto, XVII recto] THE BYZANTINE DIPTYCH

The Virgin enthroned.

Inscription: ICI EST FAITE REINE DEL CIEL.

Virgin enthroned between two archangels wearing richly decorated tunicles and carrying labara. Her hands are raised in prayer. The arrangement recalls that of the apse at Cefalù, though here the Virgin is shown standing, see O. Demus, *The Mosaics of Norman Sicily*, London 1949, pls. 1, 3.

FOLIO 31 [folio 15 verso, XVII verso] THE LAST JUDGEMENT

The Dead are awakened.

Inscription: ICI EST LA RESVRRECTION COMVNE AL IOR DE IVISE.

At the four corners of the miniature the angels blow their trumpets and the dead rise from their tombs.

FOLIO 32 [folio 16 recto, XVIII recto] THE LAST JUDGEMENT

Six Apostles.

Inscription: ICI SIENT LI APOSTLES PVR IVIER.

Six apostles seated within six triangular sections. St Peter is at the top.

FOLIO 33 [folio 16 verso, XVIII verso] THE LAST JUDGEMENT

Angels.

Inscription: ICI SVNT LI ANGLE.

Six angels in two registers bearing emblems of the Passion: Upper row: on the left the Scourge, in the middle the Crown of Thorns. Lower row: on the left the bucket for the vinegar, in the middle the spear, on the right four nails.

FOLIO 34 [folio 17 recto, XIX recto] THE LAST JUDGEMENT

The Blessed on the right hand of God.

Inscription: ICIST SERVNT LA DESTREE DEV AL IVISE.

In two registers: In the upper half a series of six rows of the heads and shoulders of men and women; in the lower part six ecclesiastics including an archbishop wearing a pallium, and three abbots.

FOLIO 35 [folio 17 verso, XIX verso] THE LAST JUDGEMENT

1　Christ in Majesty displaying his Wound.

Inscription: ICI APAREIST DEVS EHVEM EN SA MAIESTE E MVSTRE LA PLAIE DE SVN LAZ.

2　The Cross supported by two angels.

Inscription: ICI MOSTRENT LI ANGEL LI CRVIZ NOSTRE SEIGNVR.

The Cross has jewelled terminals and is held up in front of an altar.

FOLIO 36 [folio 18 recto, XX recto] THE LAST JUDGEMENT

The Apostles on the left hand.

Inscription: ICI SIENT LI AVTRE APOSTLE PVR IVGIER.

Six other apostles seated in a manner similar to those on folio 32.

FOLIO 37 [folio 18 verso, XX verso] THE LAST JUDGEMENT

The Damned on the left hand of God.

Inscription: ICIST SERVNT A LA SENESTRE DAM LE DEV AL IVISE.

In two registers. Above, heads and shoulders only in five rows. Below are six mournful looking ecclesiastics. The whole composition matches folio 34.

FOLIO 38 [folio 19 recto, XXI recto] THE LAST JUDGEMENT

The Tortures of the Damned.

Inscription: ICI EMMEINENT LI DEIABLE LES DAMNEZ EN ENFERS.

In two registers. Above three devils carry two human beings. One of them has his arms bound with an huge key. Below are various tortures. On the right devils poke down human beings into a pit.

FOLIO 39 [folio 19 verso, XXI verso] THE LAST JUDGEMENT

An Angel locks the door of Hell.

Inscription: ICI EST ENFERS E LI ANGELS KI ENFERME LES PORTES.

A wonderful representation of Hell as a great mouth within which are human beings and devils. A very similar representation is found in the New Minster Register, B. M. Stowe MS 944, folio 7, see E. G. Millar, *English Illuminated Manuscripts from the Tenth to the Thirteenth Century*, pl. 25b.

deus

4. The Death of the Virgin. Folio 29

The Miniatures: Folios 2-39

The plates are reproduced in their original sequence

5. God in the Garden of Eden and the Expulsion; Adam and Eve receive the instruments of work, and work; Cain and Abel. Folio 2

6. Noah commanded to build the Ark; the Return of the Dove;
the Sacrifice of Isaac. Folio 3

7. Moses and the Burning Bush; the Almighty with David and Solomon (?);
the Angel appearing to Joachim. Folio 4

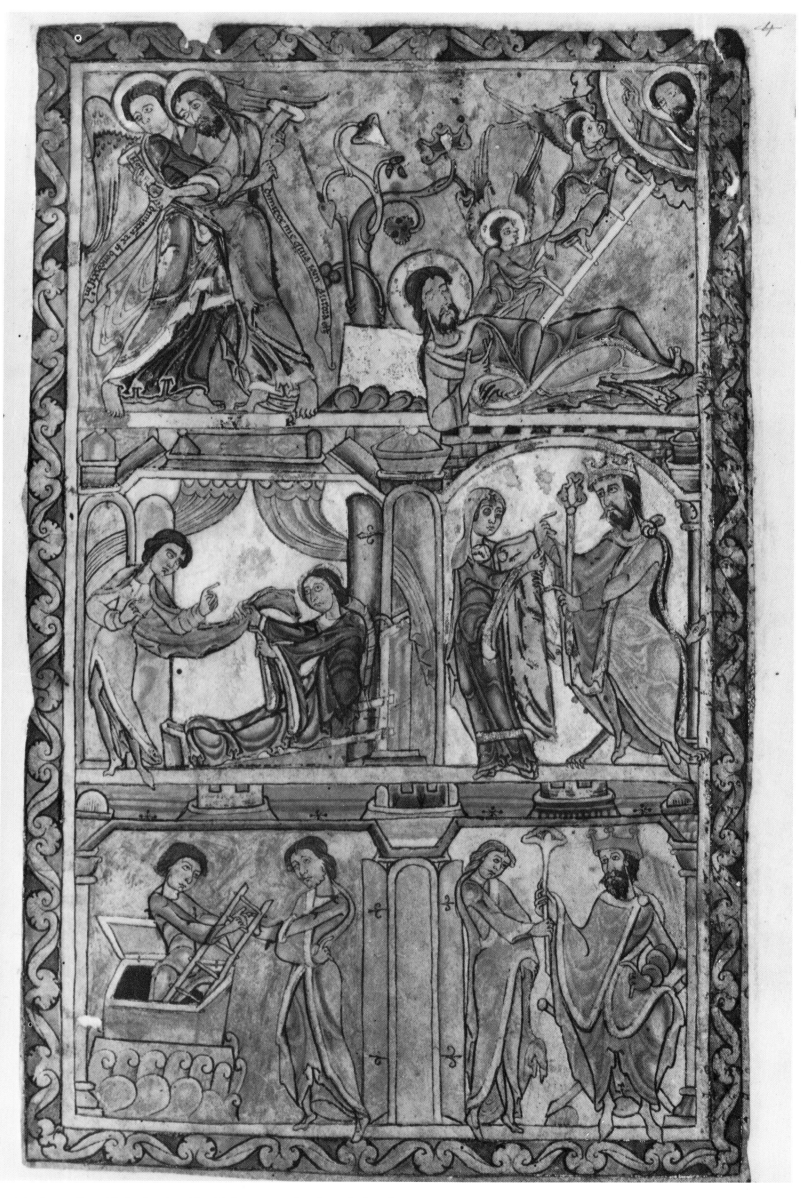

8. Jacob wrestling with the Angel, and Jacob's Dream; Joseph and Potiphar's Wife;
Joseph's Imprisonment (?), and Joseph preferred by Pharaoh. Folio 5.

9. David before Saul, and David and Goliath;
David beheads Goliath and brings the head to Saul. Folio 6

10. David rescues a Sheep from the Lion;
Anointing of David by Saul. Folio 7

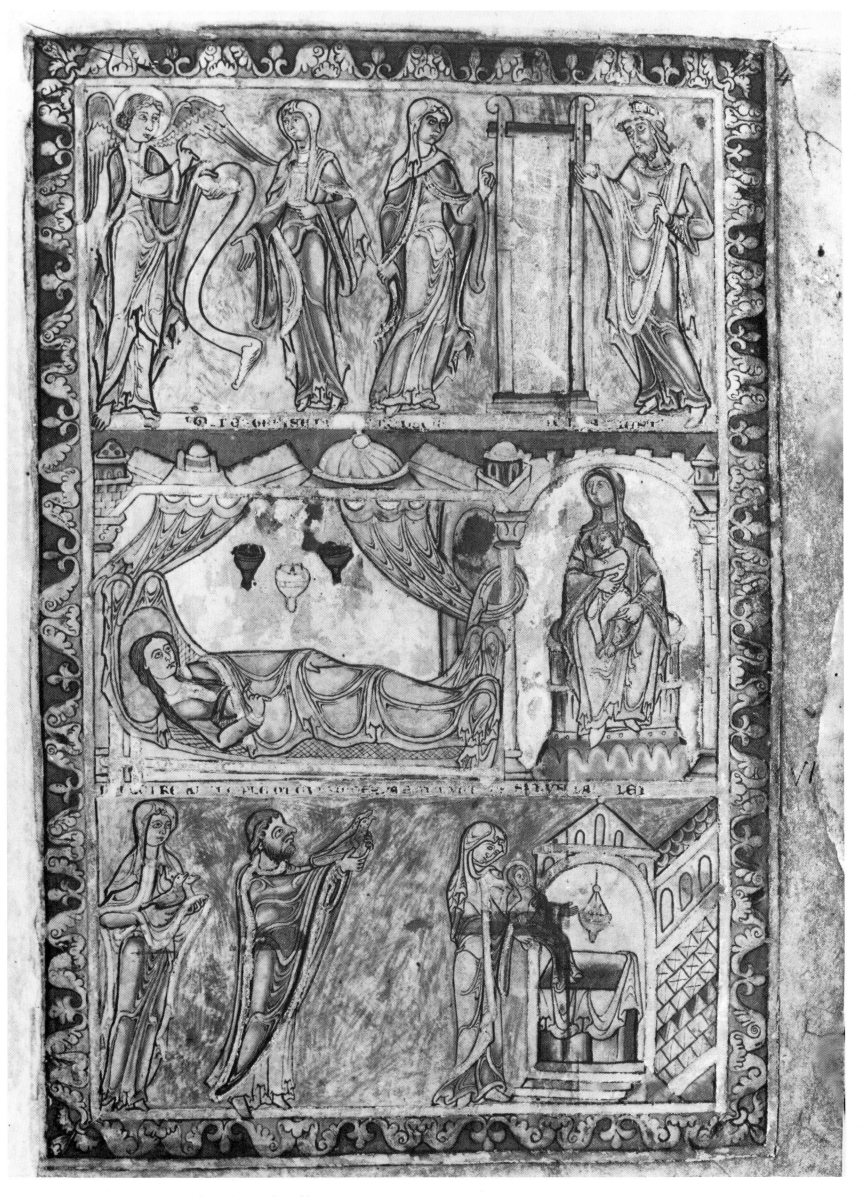

11. The Annunciation to St. Anne, and the Meeting at the Golden Gate;
the Birth of the Virgin; the Presentation of the Virgin in the Temple. Folio 8

12. The Tree of Jesse. Folio 9

13. The Angel Gabriel sent to the Virgin Mary; the Annunciation; the Visitation; the Nativity. Folio 10

ICI VIENENT LI TREI REI A HERODE:

14. The Annunciation to the Shepherds; the Magi before Herod. Folio 11

15. The Journey of the Magi to Bethlehem; the Adoration of the Magi. Folio 12

16. The Magi warned to flee from Herod; Joseph warned to go to Egypt. Folio 13

17. The Flight into Egypt; the Massacre of the Innocents. Folio 14

ICI SIET IESVS XPC EN COI LES MAISTRES DE LA LEI AL TEMPLE

18. The Presentation in the Temple; Christ among the Doctors. Folio 15

19. Mary and Joseph find Jesus in the Temple; the Baptism of Christ. Folio 16

20. The Marriage at Cana; Drawing the Water and filling the Waterpots for the Miracle. Folio 17

21. The First and Second Temptation of Christ; the Third Temptation. Folio 18

22. The Raising of Lazarus; the Entry into Jerusalem. Folio 19

23. The Last Supper; Christ washes the Feet of the Apostles. Folio 20

24. The Betrayal; the Flagellation. Folio 21

25. The Crucifixion; the Deposition. Folio 22

26. The Entombment; the Women at the Sepulchre. Folio 23

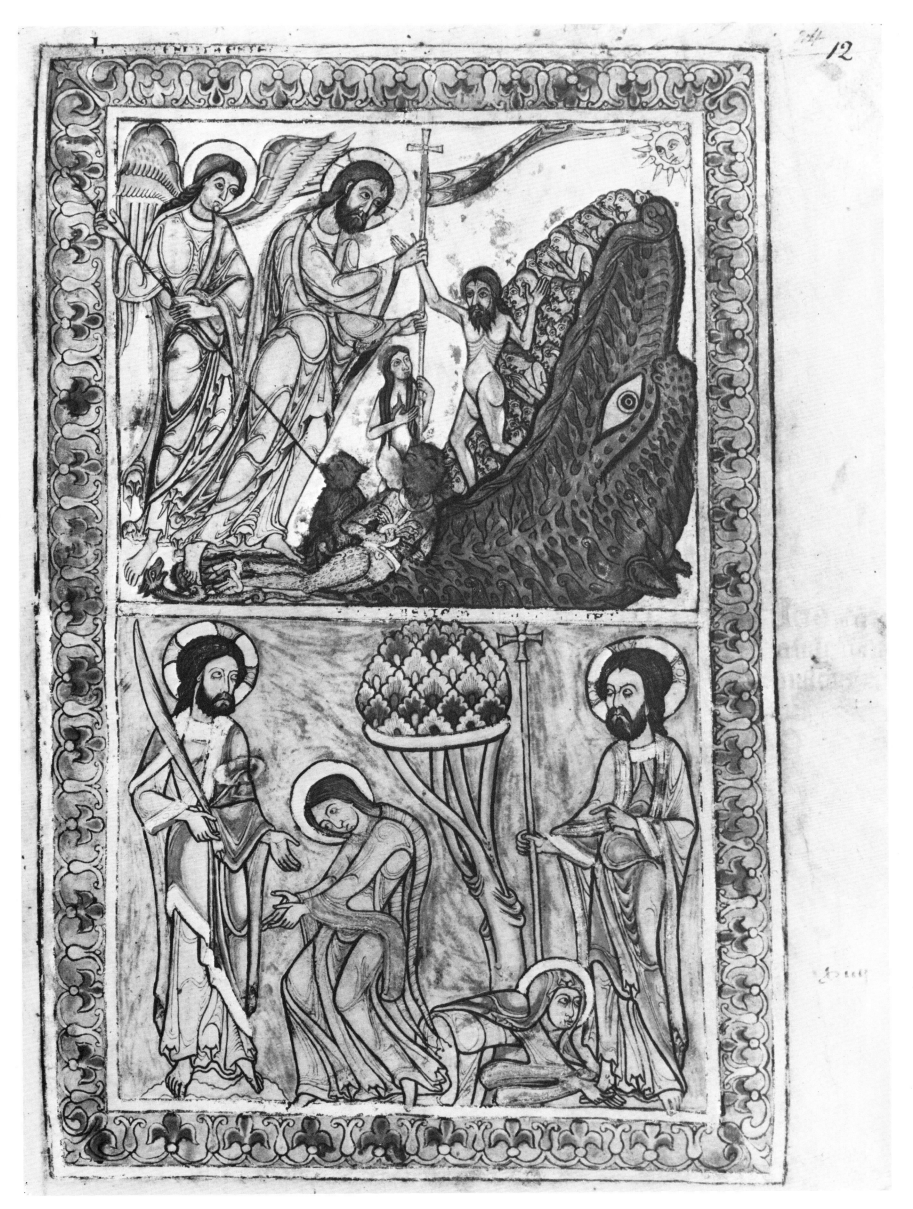

27. The Harrowing of Hell; Christ appears to Mary Magdalene. Folio 24

28. St. Peter receives the Keys; Christ and the Disciples
on the Road to Emmaus. Folio 25

29. The Supper at Emmaus; Christ appears to the Apostles
and St. Thomas touches His Wound. Folio 26

30. The Ascension. Folio 27

31. The Descent of the Holy Spirit at Pentecost; Christ in Majesty. Folio 28

ICI EST LA SVOTION DE NOSTRE DAME

deus

32. The Death of the Virgin. Folio 29

33. The Virgin Enthroned. Folio 30

34. The Awakening of the Dead. Folio 31

35. Six Apostles. Folio 32

36. Angels. Folio 33

37. The Blessed on the Right Hand of God. Folio 34

38. Christ displaying His Wound; the Cross supported by two Angels. Folio 35

39. Six Apostles. Folio 36

ICIST SERVNT A LA SENESTRE DEOO LEDEV AL IVISE:

40. The Damned on the Left Hand of God. Folio 37

41. The Tortures of the Damned. Folio 38

42. An Angel locking the Door of Hell. Folio 39

The Full-Page Miniatures

At the beginning of the manuscript are thirty-eight full-page miniatures painted on the rectos of folios 2 to 39. This does not seem to be the original arrangement which appears to have followed the usual practice of putting the pictures on the rectos and versos so that they faced one another. This can be demonstrated in the case of Nero C.IV: on most alternate leaves of the manuscript, as it is at present constituted, two sets of foliation can be seen. The first is in Arabic numerals placed in the top right hand corner of the leaf. The second set of foliation is in Roman numerals and is placed in the margin. It appears first on folio 8 as folio VI whereas the ink foliation gives it as folio 4. This suggests that between the time when the Roman numeration was made and the time when the ink Arabic numeration was added two leaves had been lost from the beginning. It is likely that they contained scenes of the Creation and the beginning of the story of Adam and Eve. The date at which these various foliations were made is not clear but the Roman numeration looks like the end of the sixteenth century. The ink Arabic numeration is later. At some time before the middle of the nineteenth century the leaves with the full-page miniatures were split and the verso pictures mounted as rectos.

These thirty-eight full-page miniatures divide roughly into three main sections. First is a scriptural series extending from folio 2 to 28; secondly the two miniatures on folios 29 and 30 of the *Death of the Virgin* and the *Virgin in Glory*, in the Byzantine style; and thirdly there is a series of *Last Judgement* pictures on folios 31 to 39. The scriptural series can be further subdivided: folios 2 to 5 contain Genesis scenes; folios 6 and 7 scenes from the *Life of David*; folios 8 and 9, the *Life of the Virgin* and the *Tree of Jesse*. From folio 10 to 28 are scenes from the *Life of Christ*, from the *Annunciation* to the *Descent of the Holy Spirit*.

The miniatures are arranged in a variety of ways. At the beginning the Genesis pictures are placed in three registers. Their similarity suggests a single source. This changes at the David pictures on folios 6 and 7 which are in two registers and on quite a different scale. Three registers are used for the *Life of the Virgin*, but these pictures have been contrived from the scenes of the *Life of Christ*. Thus the *Annunciation to St. Anne* is clearly borrowed from an *Annunciation* miniature. In the same way the *Presentation of the Virgin in the Temple* on folio 8 is a reworking of a representation of the *Presentation of Christ in the Temple*.

It is not possible to point to any single source for the Old Testament scenes. As has already been pointed out the cycle is incomplete owing to the loss of leaves at the beginning. In one or two places there seems to be a suggestion of Byzantine

69

43. An Angel hands Adam his Tool.
Paris, Bibliothèque Nationale, Ms. Gr. 510, folio 52v

44. An Angel hands Adam his Tool.
Detail of folio 2

influence: as in the presentation of the mattock to Adam as a tool of his labour by an angel, which should be compared with a similar scene in the Paris *Gregory*, folio 52 verso.[1] Rather similar to the same scenes in the Paris *Gregory* is the *Sacrifice of Isaac* on folio 3 and the two scenes of *Jacob and the Angel* and *Jacob's Ladder* on folio 5.[2] Into the Old Testament pictures a group of pictures of the *Life of David* has been introduced. Eight scenes are distributed over two consecutive folios 6 and 7. As they now stand they are in an unhistorical order. On folio 6 on the top left hand side is David refusing the armour of Saul.[3] On the right David confronts Goliath. Below on the left David brings the giant's head to Saul;[4] on the right David beheads Goliath. On the next folio, 7, the upper scene shows David seizing the sheep from the lion's mouth.[5] Below is the *Anointing of David by Samuel*.[6] All except the scene of David refusing Saul's arms are to be found in the eleventh century Psalter from Winchester, British Museum, Cotton MS Tiberius C.VI, though in a different order.[7] Here again the compositions should be compared with Byzantine representations. This is rather close in the scene of the *Anointing of David*, though it may be noted that, whereas in the medieval West the horn of oil is tipped over David's head, in the Early Christian and Byzantine versions the horn is carefully held upright.[8]

The Old Testament series of pictures is divided from the New Testament series by the pictures of the *Birth of the Virgin* and the *Tree of Jesse*; the former being probably based iconographically upon scenes from the Gospels. The New Testament series is almost entirely devoted to pictures relating to the *Nativity* and to the *Passion of Christ*. Thus both parables and miracles are omitted except for the theophanic miracles of the *Marriage of Cana* on folio 17 and the *Raising of Lazarus* on folio 19. As a series it is quite distinct from such manuscripts as

70

45 and 46. Life of David. London, British Museum, Cotton Ms. Tiberius C VI, folios 8 and 9

47. David seizing the Sheep from the Lion's Mouth. Detail of folio 7

48. Anointing of David.
Paris, Bibliothèque Nationale,
Ms. Gr. 510, folio 174

49. Anointing of David.
London, British Museum,
Cotton Ms. Tiberius C VI, folio 9v

50. Anointing of David.
Detail of folio 7

Cambridge, Pembroke MS 120 or the series of leaves, possibly from Bury St. Edmunds or Canterbury, in the British Museum, the Victoria and Albert Museum and the Pierpont Morgan Library; both of which include parables as well as miracles.[9]

Perhaps the most striking feature about these miniatures is a feeling for the grotesque which transforms the rather conventional iconography into something very individual. This feature will again be pointed out in connection with the style, but it is equally important to see how it transforms the iconography into a new image. In some respects the New Testament series is fairly close in choice of subjects to the set in the St Albans Psalter, though the iconography is certainly quite distinct from that manuscript. One of the rare scenes in Nero C. IV is on folio 10 of the *Angel Gabriel being sent to Mary*. A similar miniature is to be found in the rather earlier Shaftesbury Psalter.[10] The story of the *Disciples at Emmaus* is to be found in the St Albans Psalter as well as in Pembroke College MS 120 and the single leaf in the Victoria and Albert Museum. In Nero C. IV only two incidents are shown: the meeting with Christ on the road and the meal at Emmaus.

In many ways the *Last Judgement* which occupies folios 31 to 39 is the most interesting set of pictures. The series begins with a representation of the *Resurrection of the Dead* on folio 31. The rest of the miniatures when combined into a single composition form a splendid miniature of the *Last Judgement* in which the centre of the composition is the miniature on folio 35 of Christ seated showing his wounds, with two angels supporting the Cross below. On either side of this central theme are apostles and angels, on the right are the Blessed and on the left the Damned. Finally there is on folio 39 a superb and rightly famous picture of an

72

angel locking up the gate of Hell. It is conceivable that this miniature did not form part of the *Last Judgement* composition, but was derived from an independent representation which already appears in Winchester in the first half of the eleventh century. In the *Liber Vitae* of Hyde Abbey Winchester, now British Museum Stowe MS 944, on folio 7 is a miniature of the *Last Judgement* divided into three registers. In the lowest register is the locking up of Hell with the angel holding a great key, very like the Nero C. IV miniature, standing outside the picture. It refers to Revelation 20, 1–30: 'And I saw an angel come down from heaven, having the key of the bottomless pit and a great chain in his hand and he laid hold on the dragon, that old serpent which is the Devil and Satan and bound him a thousand years. And cast him into the bottomless pit and shut him up and set a seal upon him.'

There seems to have been some interest in *Last Judgement* scenes at Winchester. Besides Nero C. IV and the *Liber Vitae* of Hyde it was known there in the tenth century and possibly earlier. It is found in the English additions to the Athelstan Psalter in the British Museum[11] and it is possible that the painting excavated in the foundations of the New Minster by Mr Biddle in 1966 also represented a part of a *Last Judgement*.[12]

As a collection of miniatures the full-page pictures in Nero C. IV are in the tradition which was already established in Winchester in the middle of the eleventh century by such manuscripts as Tiberius C. VI and further expanded in such books as the St Albans Psalter.

51. The Angel Gabriel sent to Mary.
London, British Museum, Lansdowne Ms. 383, folio 12v

52. The Angel Gabriel sent to Mary.
Detail of folio 10

53 and 54. Christ in Majesty with Saints. London, British Museum, Cotton Ms. Galba A. XVIII, folios 2v and 21

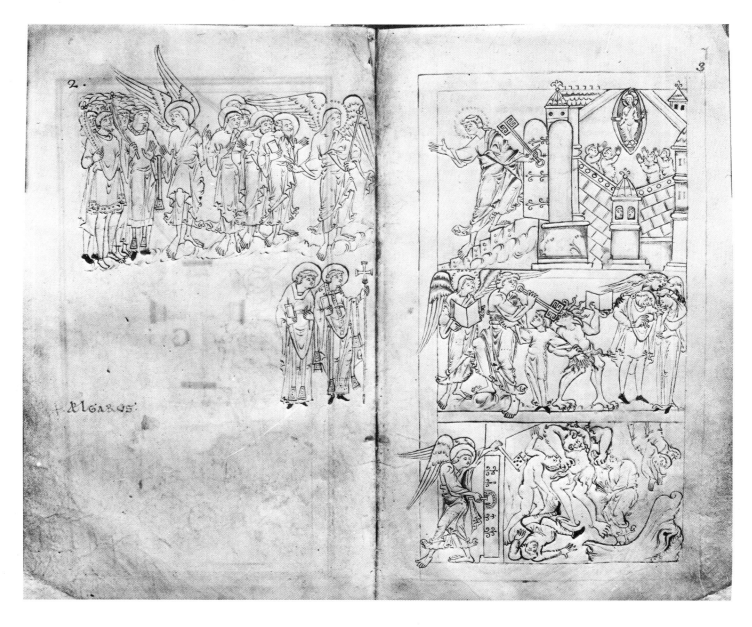

55 and 56. The Last Judgement. London, British Museum, Stowe Ms. 944, folios 6v and 7

57. The Last Judgement. Folios 31 to 39

58. Jacob's Dream. Detail of folio 5 (enlarged)

The Style of the Miniatures

There are two styles in the large miniatures of Nero C. IV. First is that found in the majority, which may conveniently be called the English style. The second is found only in the two 'Byzantine' style miniatures on folios 29 and 30, dividing the christological series from the cycle of the *Last Judgement*. The miniatures in the English style do not subdivide into various hands and can therefore be discussed all together. For the most part their colour, particularly the blue, has been removed, though heavy painting sometimes remains on the faces, as in the figure of the aged Simeon in the *Presentation in the Temple* on folio 15. Any analysis of the style is therefore based upon the treatment of the drawing.

As in most Northern Romanesque paintings there is little or no attempt to represent space or perspective. Architecture is very much like conventional stage scenery and serves as a framework within which the actors can give their performances. Thus the building which houses the *Last Supper* on folio 20 is an elaborate, though almost meaningless affair. Within the frame the figures are brought as close as possible to the edge. They are frequently allowed to stray a little way out of the frame and their feet dangle over the side. By such means the figures attain a certain measure of independence yet they are always securely attached to the picture. This can be seen clearly in the figure of the sleeping Jacob at the foot of the heavenly ladder on folio 5 where he leans over the border of the miniature as if it were a window sill. This practice of allowing the figure to cross the frontier of the picture can already be seen in the English manuscripts of the Anglo-Saxon period.[13] Movement is expressed in a similar way by cutting off part of the scene. Thus in the journey of the Magi to Bethlehem on folio 12 the front half of the foremost horse has already passed behind the frame while the tail of the third horse has not yet emerged from behind the border on the left.

There is naturally no attempt to indicate perspective or suggest distance, and the ground upon which some of the figures stand is represented by a series of conventional swirls. As has already been indicated architecture is only introduced when the scene needs it, as in the *Second Temptation* on folio 18 or when it performs the function of a frame as in the *Last Supper* on folio 20.

Several devices have been used to bring the various figures into relationships with each other. First is the use of expressive gestures accompanied by pointing and gesticulating hands. A good example of this is in the miniature of *Christ among the Doctors* on folio 15 where the learned Jews raise their hands in argument and gaze intently on their youthful opponent. Another method of bringing

59. The Last Supper. Detail of folio 20

60. The Journey of the Magi to Bethlehem. Detail of folio 12

the actors in a scene together is to join them either by overlapping one figure with another or by one figure seizing the other. This may be seen in the miniature of the *Presentation in the Temple* on folio 15 where the four figures, the servant, the Virgin, Christ and the aged Simeon are all blended in one continuous flowing line. Another revealing example is on folio 2 where the angel presents the instruments of work to Adam and Eve. The angel's body is turned in the direction of Eve who is receiving the distaff, though the angel's head is turned in the opposite direction towards Adam who is given a mattock.

Another very characteristic way of bringing the figures together is the use of scrolls. A particularly good example of this may be seen in the *Annunciation to the Shepherds* on folio 11 and also in the *Magi before Herod* on the same folio where the long sleeve of the foremost king resembles the scroll held by Herod. The *Third Temptation* on folio 18 shows a similar combination of scrolls and draperies in which an elaborate surface decoration is achieved.

Figures throughout the manuscript are similar with rather large heads, and expressive eyes under heavy brows. Many of the men have elaborate beards often divided up in a fashion which makes them resemble bunches of carrots. Sometimes they are of inordinate length as in the Magi on folio 12 or the aged Simeon on folio 15. Occasionally some of the faces are quite grotesque; particularly when evil persons are to be shown. Thus in the *Flagellation of Christ* on folio 21 the smiters are almost caricatures of villainy. Similar savagery is found in the *Betrayal* and also in the *Massacre of the Innocents* on folio 14 where one of the infants has been seized and is being devoured by a huge golly-wog like figure. In the same way devils have become horrific with their beaked noses and mouth full of teeth.

61. A King before Herod. Detail of folio 11

62. Christ in the Third Temptation. Detail of folio 18

63. King. Detail of folio 12

64. Virgin and Apostle. Detail of folio 26

65. Head of a Devil.
Detail of folio 38

66. King warned to flee from Herod.
Detail of folio 13

67. Crowd from the Betrayal. Detail of folio 21

68. Devil from the Third Temptation.
Detail of folio 18

69. The Sacrifice of Isaac.
Detail of folio 3

71. Simeon from the Presentation in the Temple.
Detail of folio 15

70. The Raising of Lazarus.
Detail of folio 19

Draperies cling tightly to the body forming a series of almond-shaped panels which with very little difficulty become abstract patterns and reduce the surface to ornament. This type of drapery can be extremely elegant as in the figure of Christ in the *Ascension* on folio 27. It is derived ultimately from Byzantine art, but is to be found in all Romanesque art as well. In Northern Europe it always had a tendency to reduce itself to pattern. It is frequently known as the damp-fold convention.[14]

This reduction of drapery folds into ornament was particularly popular in England. In another form it had already appeared in the eleventh century in such manuscripts as the Gospels of Margaret of Scotland in the Bodleian[15] and the Gospels of Judith of Flanders in the Pierpont Morgan Library in New York.[16] Here one can see that the drapery folds no longer represent material but cover the surface with a series of abstract patterns derived from folds in the stuff. These abstract folds were in the first half of the twelfth century modified by contacts with Byzantine art, with its 'damp' folds and almond-shaped panels. Already by about 1130 the 'damp' fold in a fully developed form is to be found in the Canterbury manuscript, Oxford Bodl. MS 271 where it is seen decorating a figure of Christ in Majesty.[17] This style reached its most successful point in the Bury St Edmunds Bible in Corpus Christi College, Cambridge, MS 2, made probably between 1130 and 1140. In its miniatures there is a complete mastery of the style.[18] In Nero C. IV we see the same style in a rather more mannered form. This mannerism may be seen in the *Betrayal* miniature where it is difficult to disentangle Judas from Christ. They have been reduced to a form of interlace.

The dating of the style of Nero C. IV is assisted by comparing it with the miniatures of the Sherborne Chartulary, now Add. MS 46487 in the British Museum. The figure of St John on folio 86 verso may be usefully compared with

72. St. Matthew.
New York, Pierpont Morgan Library,
Ms. 708, folio 2v

73. Moses and Aaron.
Detail from the Bury Bible. Cambridge,
Corpus Christi College, Ms. 2, folio 94r

74. Judas and Christ.
Detail of folio 21

82

that of St Joseph in the *Flight into Egypt* of Nero C. IV. The Sherborne Chartulary can be dated about 1146. Rather later, though still relevant, is the illuminated charter of David I and his grandson, Malcolm IV of Scotland, to Kelso Abbey which is dated 1159.[19] There are also two undated manuscripts which are closely related to Nero C. IV on stylistic grounds. The first is the illustrated copy of the prayers and meditations of Anselm of Canterbury which in the Middle Ages belonged to the Benedictine nunnery at Littlemore, near Oxford, and now in the Bodleian Library.[20] The style of the Anselm is rather less robust than that of the Winchester Psalter, but a comparison between such figures as the Virgin from the *Tree of Jesse* on folio 9 and that in the Anselm makes the relationship plain.

Apart from the manuscripts just discussed perhaps the closest parallels in English drawing in Nero C. IV are to be found in the work of the Master of the Leaping Figures in the Winchester Bible. Very many of the same artistic conventions were followed by both artists: the rather large heads, the expressive gestures, and above all the drapery with its almond shaped damp folds. At the same time it seems that Nero C. IV represents a slightly earlier version of it. One may compare two figures, one from each manuscript; the figure of St Peter in the *Ascension* in Nero C. IV, folio 27, and the superb drawing of St James on folio 429 of the Winchester Bible. It is clear that the latter shows the style in a more developed form.

There are two works from the continent which should be mentioned since both of them resemble the style superficially. Both come from the Plantagenet Empire. They are the paintings in the Leper Hospital of Le Petit Quevilly, near Rouen, and a Pliny's *Natural History* now at Le Mans.[21] The latter in particular has some similarity to the style of Nero C. IV: heads, beards and drapery; even the very elaborate architectural setting of the miniature of Pliny offering his

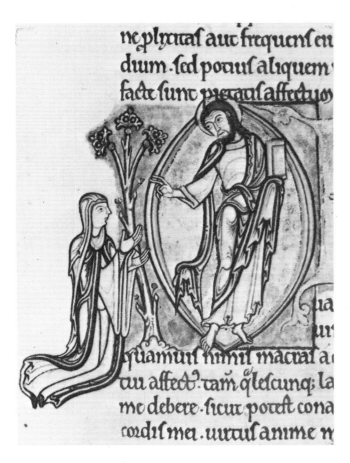

75. Illustration to the Prayers and Meditations of St. Anselm. Oxford, Bodleian Library Ms. Auct. D. 2. 6., folio 156

76. Joseph from the Flight into Egypt. Detail of folio 14

77. St. John. Sherborne Chartulary. London, British Museum, Add. Ms. 46487, folio 86v

book to the Emperor Vespasian may be compared with the pinnacles and turrets surmounting the house in which the Last Supper is held on folio 20 and in the *Pentecost* on folio 28. The Pliny has already been thought of as an import from England, and it is certainly similar to English work. There are, however, certain differences, especially in the way the drapery is tackled. Though there are the same 'damp folds' the whole treatment is overworked in the Pliny. It must also be remembered that much of the style is common to both French and English work.

Petit Quevilly was a leper hospital founded in 1183 by Henry II of England.[22] The vault of the choir of the chapel is decorated with paintings which have been dated late in the twelfth century. In many ways the style looks like a further stage of that found in Nero C. IV. The scenes are painted in roundels between which are elaborate conventional foliage. This foliage resembles that found in the Winchester Bible. At the same time the treatment shows a development pointing towards Gothic painting which is completely lacking in Nero C. IV.

78. St. James. Winchester Bible, folio 429r.
Winchester, Cathedral Library

79. St. Peter.
Detail of folio 27

84

80. Pliny offering his book to Vespasian
Le Mans, Bibliothèque Municipale. Ms. 263, folio 10

81. Pentecost. Folio 28

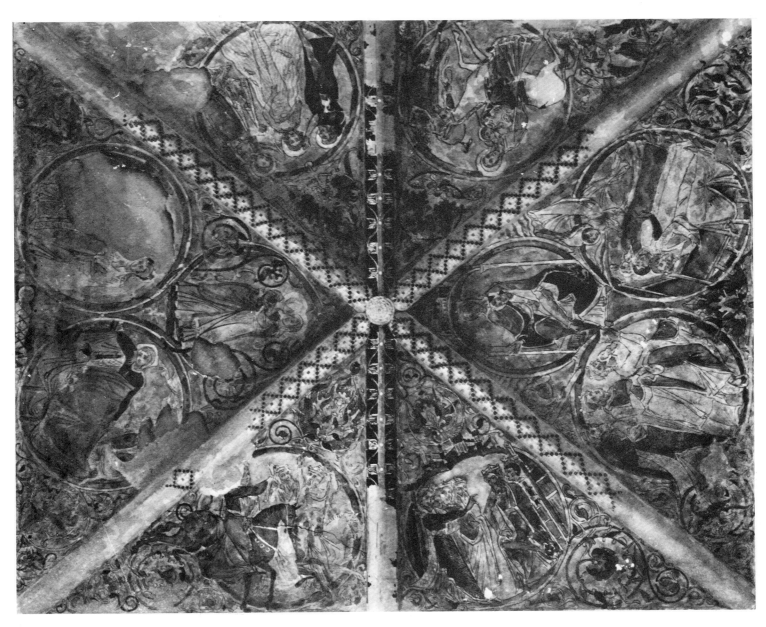

82. Choir-vaults. Chapel of the Leper Hospital, Petit-Quevilly (Seine-Maritime)

83 a, b, c. Details of the Petit-Quevilly choir-vaults

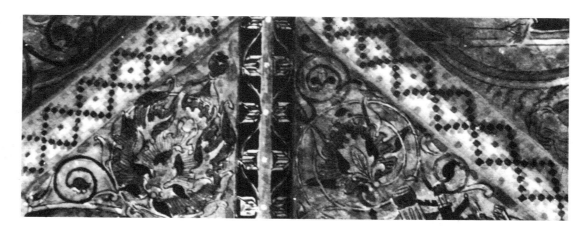

84. Foliage from the Petit-Quevilly choir-vaults

The Byzantine Diptych

Between the scriptural series of pictures and the *Last Judgement* series were two miniatures facing each other which are painted by a different hand and in a completely different style. They now occupy folios 29 and 30. If they are restored to their original arrangement they form a diptych with the *Koimesis* or *Death of the Virgin* on the left and the *Virgin in Glory* on the right. They have been described as being painted in an Italo-byzantine style, and it is true that a Mediterranean model must lie behind them. Iconographically the *Death of the Virgin* is completely Byzantine and may be compared with representations of the same subject in both icons and manuscripts. The *Virgin in Glory* shows her enthroned with her hands lifted in prayer. On either side of her are standing richly clothed angels holding *labara*. This composition may be compared with certain figures in the mosaics decorating the apses of Cefalù and Monreale.[23] The chief difference from the first is that in the Psalter the Virgin is seated and from the second the Christ child is absent.

If, however, they are carefully examined, both miniatures reveal themselves as English editions of Byzantine models. There is a linearity which suggests

85. Death of the Virgin. Detail of folio 29

87

86. Virgin in Glory. Mosaic. Monreale Cathedral

87. Virgin and Child. Mosaic. Cefalù Cathedral

ICI EST FAITE REINE DEL CIEL:

88. Virgin Enthroned. Folio 30

89. 'Wavy Ground'. Detail from the Bury Bible.
Cambridge, Corpus Christi College, Ms. 2, folio 344v

90. 'Wavy Ground'.
Detail of folio 29

English work and the curiously stylised wavy ground upon which the apostles stand in the *Koimesis* may be compared with similar conventions used in the Bury and Winchester Bibles. There is also a misunderstanding of the archetype in that the footstool which stands by the bed in the *Death of the Virgin* has in Nero C. IV been transformed into a tomb. Such a metamorphosis would be most improbable in a true work of a Mediterranean artist. It is, however, in the figure of the Virgin in prayer that the Northern origin of the miniature is clearest. The manner in which the folds of the dress are managed show a decorative tendency recalling the Bury Bible and the large hands and feet are equally revealing.

How then are these two miniatures to be explained? They are not additions and are clearly contemporary with the rest of the full-page miniatures. Until relatively recently very little has been known about Byzantine icon painting owing to the fact that so few had survived. The situation has now somewhat altered by the discovery of a large number preserved in the monastery of St Catharine on Mount Sinaï and partly published by Sotiriou and Weitzmann.[24] Some of these icons were produced in the Latin Kingdom of Jerusalem and Weitzmann has published one icon which is almost certainly by an English artist.[25] If an English icon could find its way to Mount Sinaï it is equally possible for a Byzantine diptych to find its way to Winchester and to be copied there. Historically this would be perfectly possible, particularly at Winchester where the bishop, Henry de Blois, was a well known collector of curiosities and antiques.

91. Christ in Majesty. Icon, probably by an English artist.
Mount Sinai, St. Catharine's Monastery

92. Virgin Enthroned. Detail of folio 30

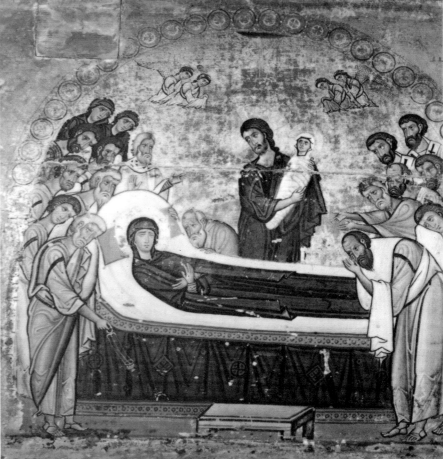

93 and 94. Icons from Mount Sinai, St. Catharine's Monastery:
The Presentation, the Descent into Limbo, the Ascension; The Death of the Virgin

chi ne alat el cunſeil deſ feluns:
et en la ueie deſ pecheurſ ne ſtout.
et en la chaere de peſtilence ne ſiſt.
aiſ en la lei de noſtre ſeignor la
uolunted. e en la ſue lei purpen
ſerat par iurn e par nuit.

iert enſement cume le fuſt qued
eſt plantet de iuſte leſ decurſ deſ
eweſ. ki dunrat ſun froit en ſon tenſ
ſa fuille ne decurrat: e tute leſ coſeſ
qʒ il unqſ ferad: ſerunt fait pſpreſ.

ient eiſſi li felun ment eiſſi: maiſ
enſement cume la puldre que li
uenz getet de la face de terre.

npurico ne ſurdent li felun en iuiſe
ne li pecheoʒ el conſeil deſ dreituriers

ar noſtre ſire cunuſt la ueie deſ iuſ
teſ: e le ire deſ felunſ perirat.

ur qi fremirent leſ genz eli po
ple purpenſerent uaineſ coſeſ:
irei de tre eſtourent: eli prince ſa
aſemblerent en un: en contre noſtre
ſeignoʒ e en contre ſun criſt.

qñ abiit in conſilio impioʒum.
& in uia peccatoʒ non ſtetit. & in
cathedra peſtilentiæ non ſedit:
ed in lege domini uoluntaſ eiuſ:
& in lege eiuſ medicabitur
die ac nocte.

t erit tanqua lignu qd plantatu
eſt ſecuſ decurſuſ aquatu: quod
fructu ſuu dabit in tempore ſuo
t foliu eiuſ non defluet: & omia
quecuq; faciet proſperabuntur

on ſic impii non ſic: ſed tanquam
puluiſ quem proicit uentuſ a
facie terre

deo non reſurgunt impii in iudicio.
neq; peccatoreſ in conſilio iuſtoʒum.

Quoniam nouit dnſ uiam iuſtoʒu:
& iter impioʒum pibit.

VARE fremuerunt genteſ &
popli meditati ſunt inania
ſtiterunt regeſ terrç & principeſ con
uenerunt in unum: aduerſuſ dnm
& aduerſuſ xpm eiuſ.

95. Initial to Psalm 1. Folio 46

The Initials

On the whole the decoration of the initials was not very lavish. Each verse of the psalm was provided with a plain coloured letter occupying the height of a single line of writing. More decorated letters occupying more space were placed at the beginning of each psalm. At some time in the thirteenth century these were embellished with a series of penwork flourishes. In three places there are beautifully drawn Romanesque letters. They are on folios 46 (Beatus vir, Ps. 1), 57 verso (Dominus illuminatio, Ps. 26), 98 (Dominus ex-audi orationem meam, Ps. 101) and are an indication that the Psalter was divided into the eightfold division. Psalm 1 has two large initials B; one for the Latin the second for the French version. That provided for the Latin section is decorated with pictures of David as the author of the Psalter. In the upper bow of the letter he is shown writing in a book, inspired by the Holy Ghost in the form of a bird. In the lower bow he is seated playing a musical instrument. David inspired by the Holy Dove was already known in Winchester in the eleventh century, appearing in a slightly different form on folio 10 of British Museum Cotton MS Tiberius C. VI.[26] An even closer parallel can be seen in the initial at the opening of the St Albans Psalter in Hildesheim.[27] For the French version only ornament has been used. The two bows which are decorated with leaf scrolls of great magnificence are joined by a beast's mask.

The smaller Romanesque initials on folio 57 verso and 98 recto have a characteristic rather sprawling leaf ornament which stretches out into octopus-like tentacles. On folio 98 recto this leaf is combined with two vigorously drawn dragons. Similar beasts and ornament can be found in the Bury and Winchester Bibles.[28] The ornament should also be compared with the ornament of the initials in the Winchester Chartulary in the British Museum, Add. MS 15350. In many ways they resemble most closely some in the Winchester Bible.[29]

The illustrations that follow, 96–102, are reproduced in considerable enlargement.

96–97. Leaf-scroll ornament in Initial B. Folio 46

98–99. David writing; David playing his Instrument. Details from Initial B. Folio 46

ego aute inii noc
fui fu. redime m

Pet mi stetit in di
benedicam te do

NS illum
mea que
Domi
mee. aquo trep

100. Leaf-scroll from folio 57v

on auertaf faciem t
quacuma; die tribu

101. Initial D. Folio 98r

Ip
L
S

face de mee. en c
fur trauaille en

102. Initial S. Folio 98r

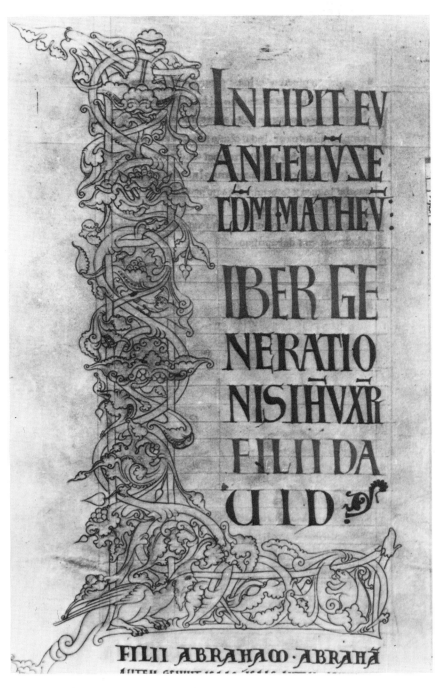

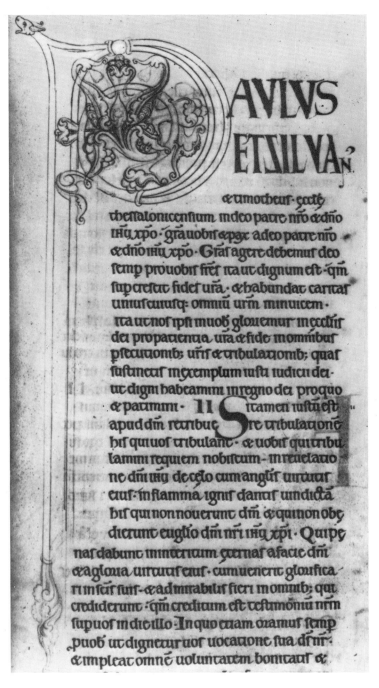

103 and 104. Initials from the Winchester Bible, folios 376v and 456r. Winchester, Cathedral Library

105. Leaf-scroll ornament from the Bury Bible.
Cambridge, Corpus Christi College, Ms. 2, folio 375r

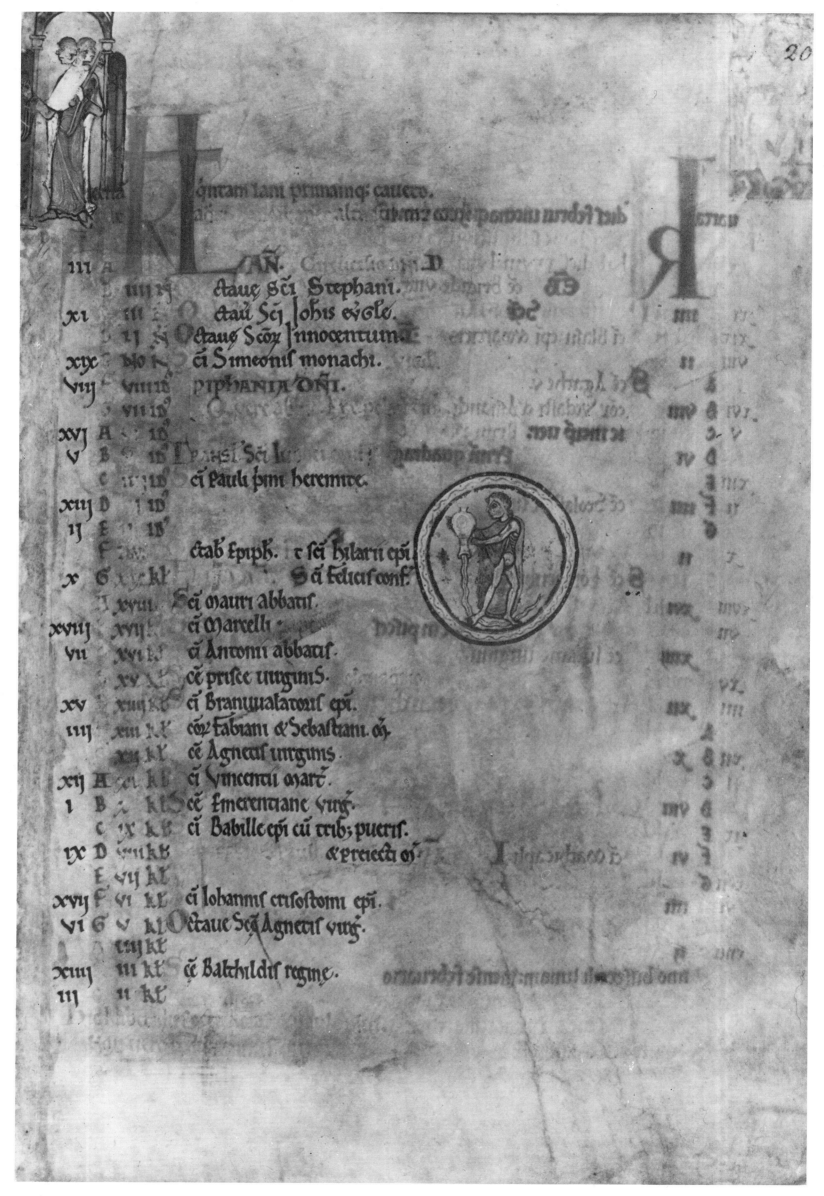

őntam iam prima qs̄ caucto.

dat febrm uteroq̄ quea ereseut...

KL̄ AÑ.

iii	A			
	B	iiii		ctaue Sc̄i Stephani.
xi		iii		ctau Sc̄i Iohīs euāgle.
		ii		Octaue Scōr Innocentum.
xix		id		c̄i Simeonis monachi.
viii	f	uiiii		PIPHANIA DÑI.
		uiii id		
xvj	A	uii id		Transl̄ Sc̄i
v	B	ui id		c̄i Pauli p̄mi heremite.
	C	u id		
xiiij	D	iiii id		
ij	E	iii id		
		ii id		ctab Epiph. e sc̄i hilarii epī
x	G	idus		Sc̄i felicis conf.
		xviiii		Sc̄i Mauri abbatis.
xviij		xvij		c̄i Marcelli
vii		xui kl̄		c̄i Antonii abbatis.
		xu kl̄		cē prisce uirginis.
xv		xiiii kl̄		c̄i Branualatour epī.
iiij		xiii kl̄		cōr fabiani e Sebastiani.
		xii kl̄		cē Agnetis uirginis.
xij	A	xi kl̄		c̄i Vincentii mart̄.
i	B	x kl̄		cē Emerentiane uirḡ.
	C	ix kl̄		c̄i Babille epī cū trib; pueris.
ix	D	uiii kl̄		e p̄iecti m̄.
	E	uii kl̄		
xvij	F	ui kl̄		c̄i Iohannis crisostomi epī.
vi	G	u kl̄		Octaue Sc̄e Agnetis uirḡ.
	A	iiii kl̄		
xiiij		iii kl̄		cē Balthildis regine.
iij		ii kl̄		

uno bis... lumine... eute februario

106. Calendar Page: January. Folio 40r

The Calendar Pictures

As is the custom in many medieval calendars two series of pictures were attached to each month; the first depicting the Labours of the Months and the second the Signs of the Zodiac. Often the Labours of the Months stand at the top of the page and are associated with the KL. monogram at the beginning of the month. The Zodiac are usually lower down on the page. In Nero C. IV the signs for July and August are missing, probably because there was not enough space to include them.

The Labours are as follows:

January	A man with two heads holding a long key in his left hand and holding on to a door ring with his right hand. A rather similar figure is to be found in the Shaftesbury Psalter, British Museum Lansdowne MS 383, see J. C. Webster, *The Labors of the Months*, 1938, pl. lxii.
February	A man warming his hands at a fire.
March	A man sowing.
April	A figure holding a plant.
May	A man riding and flying his hawk.
June	A man with a scythe.
July	A man reaping with a sickle.
August	A man threshing; his flail has disappeared.
September	A man pruning.
October	A man beating down acorns for his pig.
November	Killing the pig.
December	A man seated at a table feasting.

Both the Labours of the Months and the Zodiac are painted in a much heavier manner than are the large miniatures. Though they certainly show the same style and are of the same date they are rather coarser in execution and therefore may be by another hand. However it must be remembered that the heavy painting of faces as found in the calendar pictures may be seen in some of the large miniatures as in the *Women at the Sepulchre* on folio 23.

The illustrations of the Calendar Pictures that follow are reproduced in considerable enlargement.

107. January: Man with two Heads. Folio 40r

108. February: Man warming his Hands by the Fire. Folio 40v

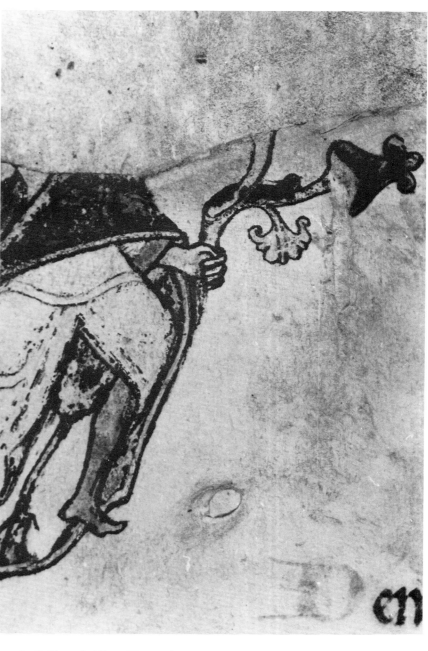

109. March: Man sowing. Folio 41r

110. April: Figure holding a Plant. Folio 41v

111. May: Man riding and flying his Hawk. Folio 42r

112. June: Man with Scythe. Folio 42v

113. July: Man reaping. Folio 43r

114. August: Man threshing. Folio 43v

115. September: Man pruning. Folio 44r

116. October: Man beating down acorns for his Pig. Folio 44v

117. November: Killing the Pig. Folio 45r

118. December: Man feasting. Folio 45v

119. Aquarius. Folio 40r

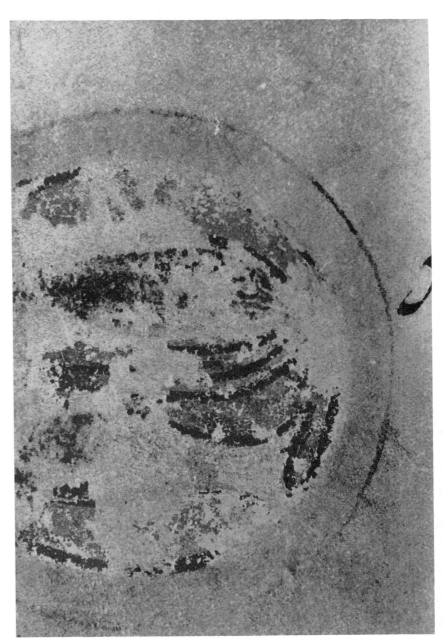

120. Pisces. Folio 40v

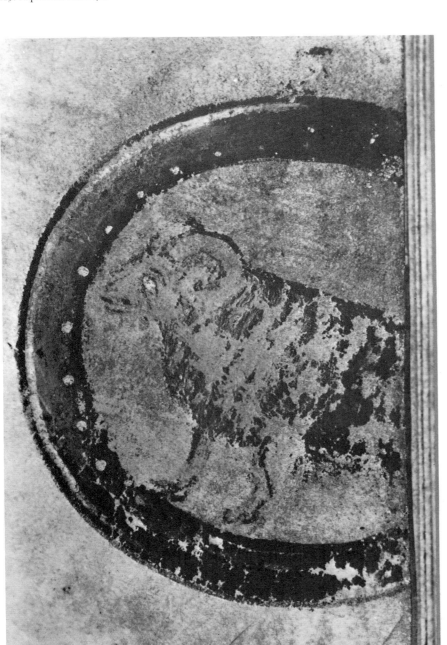

121. Aries. Folio 41r

122. Taurus. Folio 41v

123. Gemini. Folio 42r
124. Cancer. Folio 42v

125. Libra. Folio 44r
126. Scorpio. Folio 44v

127. Sagittarius. Folio 45r

128. Capricorn. Folio 45v

... romanet h ce sub gemini tacet illa.

MA IVM

Sci Athanasii epi.

Inuentio sce crucis.

Sci Iohis euuangliste ante porta latina.

Sci Victoris orz.

Translatio Sci Nicholai epi.

Scor Gordiani et Epimachi oog.

Sci Maioli abbatis.

Scor Nerei Achillei et Pancratii o.

Sce Eadwage 9

IVNII

Sci Dunstani archi epi.

Vltimu tinu rogat.

Sci Vrbani pape et oog.

Hic cepta fuit seclusio carte Ade regis de Lucintune.

Sce Petronelle virg   ic habet

dies hor. xvi et paulo pl.

129. Calendar Page: May. Folio 42r

The Calendar

The calendar which is found on folios 40 recto to 45 verso is similar in pattern to other medieval calendars. There are columns of Golden Numbers and Sunday Letters followed by the normal Latin dates. At the head of each month are written couplets the first referring to the two unlucky days in each month: the Dies Aegyptiaci; the second to the appropriate sign of the Zodiac. The same set of verses is to be found added in a hand of about A.D. 1200 to the calendar of Giso of Wells in B.M. Cotton MS Vitellius A.XVIII and also in a fragment of a Winchester calendar in Westminster Abbey CC.24. These couplets are followed by notes giving the number of days in the months and the number of days in the lunar month. At the foot of each month there is a note about the number of hours in the day and night. Each month is provided with a small painting of the Labours of the Months. Most months have also a representation of the Sign of the Zodiac appropriate to the month, though these are not found for July and August.

As with most calendars the main basis is Roman. Naturally a number of English saints appear. The general picture which evolves from the entries suggests a Winchester origin, though it is not possible to say definitely whether it represents Hyde Abbey or the Cathedral. The following entries should be mentioned: 9th January Translation of St Judoc; 12th March Aelfege, bishop of Winchester; 15th June Eadburga, virgin, buried at the Nunnaminster at Winchester; 8th July Grimbald, confessor, whose shrine was at Hyde; 15th July Translation of St Swithun, written in several colours; 2nd August Aethelwold; 4th September Translation of SS Cuthbert and Birinus; 10th September Translation of St Aethelwold; 30th October Ordination of St Swithun; 4th November Brinstan, bishop of Winchester; 3rd December Birinus, apostle of the South Saxons. Besides these mainly Winchester worthies two feasts are singled out for special veneration. The first is St Valentine on 14th February whose name is written in capitals; the second is St Denys and his companions on 9th October who is also in capitals and has been provided with an octave. Both these feasts had some importance at Hyde. There are two feasts which do not appear in other Winchester calendars: 29th April, Hugh, abbot of Cluny written in green and Maiolus, abbot, on 11th May. Both are Cluniac saints and were introduced into the Winchester calendar presumably by the personal direction of Henry de Blois, who as a young man had been a monk of Cluny and maintained a connection with that great house.

What we have then is a calendar made for use at Winchester by the bishop, Henry de Blois. The Benedictine element is easily explained by the fact that the bishop was a monk and the Winchester element is equally clear.

At some time during the thirteenth century a number of additions were made to the calendar. These are: 13th February Translatio S Eduuardi; 18th February Aduentus S Eduuardi; 18th March Passio S Eduuardi; 3rd April S Ricardi episcopi Cycestrie; 9th June Translatio S Edmundi archiepiscopi; 20th June Festiuitas S Eduuardi regis et martiris; 21st June In ueneratione reliquiarum; 3rd July Translatio S Thome apostoli; 7th July Translatio S Thome martiris; 6th August Transfiguratio domini. In addition to these there is a note on folio 41 verso commemorating the dedication of the abbey church at Shaftesbury by Anselm, archbishop of Canterbury. All these additional entries point to their having been made at Shaftesbury. The various feasts of St Edward, king and martyr, are particularly indicative as is the feast of the relics on 21st June. All these are to be found in the Shaftesbury Abbey calendar in the prayer-book in the Fitzwilliam Museum at Cambridge. These Shaftesbury additions to the calendar of Nero C. IV are all written in the same hand in red and can be dated after 1257 from the fact that the obit of Stephen Bauceyn appears on 4th June. He was a knight of King Henry III who was killed by the Welsh on 4th June 1257. It is likely that his obit was recorded at Shaftesbury because he was connected with one Juliana Bauceyn who died in 1279 as abbess of the house.

EDITORIAL NOTE

The text of the Calendar on pp. 109–120 is an edited version of the original, in which abbreviations, punctuation and arrangement have been standardized. Liturgical entries (except Vigils) which are written in blue, green or red are distinguished from those written in black by the letters *b*, *gr* and *r*. Coloured passages which are more or less illegible in the manuscript even under ultra-violet light have, where possible, been restored with the help of English calendars printed by Professor Wormald elsewhere. The set of couplets on the *dies aegyptiaci* and the Zodiac have been restored after the text added *circa* A.D. 1200 in the upper margins of an 11th-century calendar ascribed to Wells, Co. Somerset, under Bishop Giso, A.D. 1061–1088. See B.M., Cotton MS. Vitellius A.XVIII, folios 3 recto–8 verso, printed by Professor Wormald in *English Kalendars before A.D. 1100*, vol. I (Henry Bradshaw Society lxxii, 1934), pp. 100–111. The proofs of the text of the Calendar have been corrected by Professor Julian Brown, who accepts full responsibility for whatever errors may be found there.

Vicenam quintam Iani primamque caueto.
Rorat aquarius hanc manet altera sub capricorno.
Ianuarius habet dies .xxxi. luna .xxx.

1	KL.		Ianuarii.	Circumcisio Domini (r).	Dies.
2	iv	Non.	Octaue S. Stephani.		
3	iii	Non.	Octaue S. Johannis evangeliste.		
4	ii	Non.	Octaue SS. Innocentium.		
5	Non.		S. Simeonis monachi.	VIGILIA.	
6	viii	Id.	EPIPHANIA DOMINI (gr).		
7	vii	Id.	LXX per clauem terminus.		
8	vi	Id.			
9	v	Id.	TRANSLATIO S. IVDOCI CONF. (r).		
10	iv	Id.	S. Pauli primi heremite.		
11	iii	Id.			
12	ii	Id.			
13	Idus		Octabas Epiphanie; et S. Hilarii ep.		
14	xix	kl.	Februarii.	S. Felicis conf.	
15	xviii	kl.	S. Mauri abbatis.		
16	xvii	kl.	S. Marcelli [pape].		
17	xvi	kl.	S. Antonii abbatis.		
18	xv	kl.	S. Prisce v.	Sol in aquario.	
19	xiv	kl.	S. Branuualatoris ep.		
20	xiii	kl.	SS. Fabiani et Sebastiani mm.		
21	xii	kl.	S. Agnetis v.		
22	xi	kl.	S. Vincentii m.		
23	x	kl.	S. Emerentiane v.		
24	ix	kl.	S. Babille ep. cum tribus pueris.		
25	viii	kl.	CONVERSIO S. Pauli (r); et Preiecti m.		
26	vii	kl.			
27	vi	kl.	S. Iohannis crisostomi ep.		
28	v	kl.	Octaue S. Agnetis v.		
29	iv	kl.			
30	iii	kl.	S. Balthildis regine.		
31	ii	kl.			

Hic habet dies octo et paulo plus,
Nox uero paulo minus quam .xvi.

Additions
  7. Obitus Vere abbatis.

Quarta dies februi uicenaque sexta timetur.
Rorat aquarius hanc, sub piscibus illa tenetur.
Februarius habet dies .xxviii. luna .xxix.

1	KL.		Februarii.	S. Brigide v.
2	iv	Non.	PVRIFICATIO S. MARIE (r).	
3	iii	Non.	S. Blasii ep. et m.	Dies.
4	ii	Non.		
5	Non.		S. Agathe v.	
6	viii	Id.	SS. Vedasti et Amandi.	
7	vii	Id.	Hic incipit ver.	Primus terminus XL.
8	vi	Id.	Primus quadragesime.	
9	v	Id.		
10	iv	Id.	S. Scolastice v.	
11	iii	Id.		
12	ii	Id.		
13	Idus		S. Eormenhilde.	
14	xvi	kl.	Marcii.	S. VALENTINI M. (r).
15	xv	kl.	Vltimus terminus XL.	Sol in pisces.
16	xiv	kl.	S. Iuliane v.	
17	xiii	kl.		
18	xii	kl.		
19	xi	kl.		
20	x	kl.		
21	ix	kl.		
22	viii	kl.	CATHEDRA S. PETRI AP. (r).	
23	vii	kl.		
24	vi	kl.	S. Mathie ap.	Locus bissexti.
25	v	kl.	Dies.	
26	iv	kl.		
27	iii	kl.		
28	ii	kl.		

Anno bissextili lunam mense februario
Triginta cogit dierum computare sanctio
D. . . . vacillare ratio.
Et habet dies horas .x. et paulo plus,
Nox autem paulo minus quam :xiii. (sic).

Additions
13. Translatio S. Eduuardi reg. et m. (r).
18. Aduentus S. Eduuardi reg. et m. (r).

Prima necat marcii quartamque a fine timemus.
Istius pisces, aries ius optinet huius.
Martius habet dies .xxxi. luna .xxx.

1	KL.		Martii.	S. Albini ep. et conf. Dies.
2	vi	Non.		
3	v	Non.		
4	iv	Non.		
5	iii	Non.		Hic incipit .vii. embolismus.
6	ii	Non.		Hic incipit .iii. embolismus ogdoadis.
7	Non.		SS. Perpetue et Felicitatis mm.	
8	viii	Id.		Prima incensio lune paschalis.
9	vii	Id.		
10	vi	Id.		
11	v	Id.		Quere abhinc pasche terminum per clauem termin'.
12	iv	Id.	S. Gregorii [pape]; et S. Aelfegi ep.	
13	iii	Id.		
14	ii	Id.		Vltimus quadragesime.
15	Idus			
16	xvii	kl.	Aprilis.	
17	xvi	kl.		
18	xv	kl.		Primus dies seculi. Sol in ariete.
19	xiv	kl.		
20	xiii	kl.	S. Cuthberti ep.	
21	xii	kl.	S. Benedicti abbatis.	Equinoctium.
22	xi	kl.		Primum pascha et sedes epactarum.
23	x	kl.		
24	ix	kl.		Locus concurrentium.
25	viii	kl.	s. marie annuntiatio (r).	
26	vii	kl.		Dominus in sepulchro.
27	vi	kl.	resvrrectio xpi. (gr).	
28	v	kl.		
29	iv	kl.		
30	iii	kl.		
31	ii	kl.		

Hic habet dies horas .xii. et paulo plus,
Nox uero paulo minus quam duodecim.

Additions
18. Passio S. Eduuardi reg. et m. (r).

111

Denam et uicenam aprilis scito esse nociuam.
Possidet hanc aries, taurus sibi uendicat illam.
Aprilis habet dies .xxx. luna .xxix.

1	KL.		Aprilis.
2	iv	Non.	S. Marie Egyptiace.
3	iii	Non.	Hic finit .vii. embolismus.
4	ii	Non.	S. Ambrosii ep. et conf.
5	Non.		Vltima incensio lune pasche.
6	viii	Id.	Prima accensio lune rogationum.
7	vii	Id.	
8	vi	Id.	
9	v	Id.	
10	iv	Id.	
11	iii	Id.	S. Guthlaci conf.
12	ii	Id.	
13	Idus		
14	xviii	kl.	Maii. Tiburcii sociorumque eius.
15	xvii	kl.	
16	xvi	kl.	
17	xv	kl.	Sol in taurum.
18	xiv	kl.	Vltimus terminus pasche.
19	xiii	kl.	S. Aelfegi ep.
20	xii	kl.	S. Victoris pape et m.
21	xi	kl.	
22	x	kl.	S. Gaii pape et m.
23	ix	kl.	S. Georgii m.
24	viii	kl.	
25	vii	kl.	S. Marci ev.
26	vi	kl.	S. Marcellini pape et m.
27	v	kl.	S. Anastasi.
28	iv	kl.	S. Vitalis m.
29	iii	kl.	S. Hugonis abbatis (gr).
30	ii	kl.	S. Herchenuualdi ep.

Hic habet dies .xiiii. horas et paulo plus,
Nox uero habet paulo minus quam .x.

Additions

3 S. Ricardi ep. Cycestrie (r).

14 Dedicacio ecclesie monasterii Schestonie celebrata a beato Anselmo
   Cantuariensis (sic) archiepiscopo in honore Assumpcionis gloriose uirginis
   Marie (r).

25 et letania maior (r).

Tercia de maio nocet et uicesima quinta.
Sub tauro manet hec et sub geminis latet illa.
Maius habet dies .xxxi. luna .xxx.

1 KL.		Maii.	Apostolorum Philippi et Iacobi (gr, r).
2 vi	Non.	S. Athanasii ep.	
3 v	Non.	INVENTIO s. Crucis (gr).	Dies.
4 iv	Non.		
5 iii	Non.		
6 ii	Non.	S. Iohannis evangeliste ante portam latinam.	
7 Non.			
8 viii	Id.	S. Victoris m.	
9 vii	Id.	Translatio S. Nicholai ep.	
10 vi	Id.	SS. Gordiani et Epimachi mm.	
11 v	Id.	S. Maioli abbatis.	
12 iv	Id.	SS. Nerei, Achillei et Pancracii mm.	
13 iii	Id.		
14 ii	Id.		
15 Idus			
16 xvii	kl.	Iunii.	
17 xvi	kl.		
18 xv	kl.	Sol in geminis.	
19 xiv	kl.	S. Dunstani archiepiscopi.	
20 xiii	kl.		
21 xii	kl.		
22 xi	kl.		
23 x	kl.	Vltimus terminus rogationum.	
24 ix	kl.		
25 viii	kl.	S. Vrbani [pape] et m.	Dies.
26 vii	kl.	S. Augustini anglorum apostoli (r).	
27 vi	kl.		
28 v	kl.		
29 iv	kl.		
30 iii	kl.	Vltimus dominicus rogationum.	
31 ii	kl.	S. Petronelle v.	

Hic habet dies horas .xvi. et paulo plus,
Nox uero paulo minus quam .viii.

Additions
29 Hic comperta fuit seductio carte Ade Nigri de Ludintune.

Dena necat iunii, quindena a fine minatur.
Vtraque sub geminis occidit et insidiatur.
Iunius habet dies .xxx. luna .xxix.

1 KL.		Iunii.	S. Nichomedis m.
2 iv	Non.		SS. Marcellini et Petri mm.
3 iii	Non.		
4 ii	Non.		
5 Non.			S. Bonefacii ep. et m.
6 viii	Id.		
7 vii	Id.		
8 vi	Id.		
9 v	Id.		SS. Primi et Feliciani mm.
10 iv	Id.		
11 iii	Id.		S. Barnabe apostoli (r).
12 ii	Id.		SS. Basilidis, Cirini, Naboris et Nazarii.
13 Idus			
14 xviii	kl.	Iulii.	S. Basilii ep.
15 xvii	kl.		S. EADBVRGE V. (gr). SS. Viti et Modesti (r).
16 xvi	kl.		SS. Cirici et Julitte mm. Dies.
17 xv	kl.		Sol in cancro.
18 xiv	kl.		SS. Marci et Marcelliani mm.
19 xiii	kl.		SS. Geruasii et Protasii mm.
20 xii	kl.		
21 xi	kl.		S. Leutfredi abbatis.
22 x	kl.		S. Albani m.
23 ix	kl.		S. Aetheldrithe v.
24 viii	kl.		NATIVITAS S. IOHANNIS BAPTISTE (gr, r, b).
25 vii	kl.		
26 vi	kl.		SS. Iohannis et Pauli (r).
27 v	kl.		
28 iv	kl.		S. Leonis [pape].
29 iii	kl.		NATALIS SS. PETRI ET PAVLI (b, r, gr).
30 ii	kl.		S. Pauli commemoratio.

Hic habet dies horas paulo minus quam .xviii.,
Nox uero paulo plus quam .vi.

Additions
 4 Obiit Stephanus Bauceyn (r).
 9 Translatio S. Edmundi archiepiscopi (r).
13 Translatio S. Bartholomei apostoli (r).
20 Festiuitas S. Eduuardi reg. et m. (r).
21 In ueneratione reliquiarum (r).

Tredecima in iulio et uicena secunda nocebit.
Subditur hec cancro, supponitur illa leoni.
Iulius habet dies .xxxi. luna .xxx.

1	KL.		Iulii. Octaue S. Iohannis baptiste.
2	vi	Non.	Processi et Martiniani. S. Swithuni.
3	v	Non.	
4	iv	Non.	S. Martini Translatio et Ordinatio.
5	iii	Non.	
6	ii	Non.	SS. Apostolorum Octaue.
7	Non.		S. Hedde ep.
8	viii	Id.	S. GRIMBALDI CONF. (r).
9	vii	Id.	
10	vi	Id.	SS. Septem fratrum.
11	v	Id.	S. BENEDICTI abbatis Translatio.
12	iv	Id.	
13	iii	Id.	Dies.
14	ii	Id.	Incipiunt dies caniculares.
15	Idus		Translatio S. Swithuni ep. (gr, b).
16	xvii	kl.	Augusti.
17	xvi	kl.	S. Kenelmi m.
18	xv	kl.	S. Benedicti octaue. Sol in leone.
19	xiv	kl.	
20	xiii	kl.	S. Margarete v.; et S. Wlmari conf.
21	xii	kl.	S. Praxedis v.
22	xi	kl.	S. MARIE Magdalene (r); et Wandregisili abbatis. Dies.
23	x	kl.	S. Apollinaris m.
24	ix	kl.	S. Cristine v. VIGILIA.
25	viii	kl.	S. IACOBI APOSTOLI (b).
26	vii	kl.	
27	vi	kl.	SS. Septem dormientium.
28	v	kl.	S. Pantaleonis m.
29	iv	kl.	SS. Felicis, Simplicii, Faustini et Beatricis.
30	iii	kl.	SS. Abdon et Sennes. Saltus lune.
31	ii	kl.	

Hic habet dies horas paulo minus quam .xvi.,
Nox autem paulo plus quam .viii.

Additions
  3 Translatio S. Thome apostoli (r).
  7 Translatio S. Thome m. (r).

Augusti prima simul et tricena cauenda est.
Hanc leo perstringit, sub signo uirginis illa est.
Augustus habet dies .xxxi. luna .xxix. (sic).

1	KL.		Augusti. AD VINCVLA S. PETRI (gr).	Dies.
2	iv	Non.	S. Stephani [pape] et m. S. Adelwoldi ep.	
3	iii	Non.	S. Stephani et sociis eius inuentio.	
4	ii	Non.		
5	Non.		S. Osuualdi regis et m.	
6	viii	Id.	S. Syxti pape et SS. Felicissimi et Agapiti.	
7	vii	Id.	S. Donati ep. et m.	
8	vi	Id.	S. Ciriaci diaconi cum sociis suis.	
9	v	Id.	S. Romani m. VIGILIA.	
10	iv	Id.	S. LAVRENTII LEVITE ET M. (b).	
11	iii	Id.	S. Tiburcii m.; et S. Taurini ep.	
12	ii	Id.		
13	Idus		S. Ypoliti m.	
14	xix	kl.	Septembris. S. Eusebii presbiteri. VIGILIA.	
15	xviii	kl.	ASSUMPTIO S. MARIE V. (b, r, gr).	
16	xvii	kl.		
17	xvi	kl.	S. Laurentii octaue.	
18	xv	kl.	S. Agapiti m. Sol in uirgine.	
19	xiv	kl.	S. Magni m.	
20	xiii	kl.		
21	xii	kl.		
22	xi	kl.	Octaue S. MARIE; et SS. Timothei; et Simphoriani.	
23	x	kl.	S. Apollinaris m. VIGILIA.	
24	ix	kl.	S. Bartholomei apostoli (b); et S. Audoeni ep. (r).	
25	viii	kl.		
26	vii	kl.		
27	vi	kl.	S. Rufi m.	
28	v	kl.	S. Augustini ep.; et Hermetis m.	
29	iv	kl.	S. Iohannis Decollatio (r); et Sabine v.	
30	iii	kl.	SS. Felicis et Audacti mm. Dies.	
31	ii	kl.	S. Aidani ep.	

Hic habet dies paulo minus quam .xiiii. horas,
Nox uero paulo plus quam .x.

Additions
6 Transfiguratio domini (r).

Tercia septembris nocet et uicesima prima.
Virgo possidet hanc, illam retinet sibi libra.
September habet dies .xxx. luna .xxx.

1	KL.		Septembris.	S. Egidii abbatis; et Prisci m.
2	iv	Non.	Hic. . . .	
3	iii	Non.	Ordinatio S. Gregorii [pape].	Dies.
4	ii	Non.	SS. Birini et Cuthberti translatio.	
5	Non.		S. Berchtini abbatis.	
6	viii	Id.		
7	vii	Id.		
8	vi	Id.	NATIVITAS S. MARIE V. (b, gr, r).	
9	v	Id.	S. Gorgonii m.	
10	iv	Id.	S. Atheluuoldi ep. Translatio.	
11	iii	Id.	SS. Proti et Iacincti mm.	
12	ii	Id.		
13	Idus			
14	xviii	kl.	Octobris.	Exaltatio S. Crucis (gr, b).
15	xvii	kl.	S. Nicomedis m.	
16	xvi	kl.	S. Eufemie v. SS. Lucie et Geminiani.	
17	xv	kl.	S. Lamberti ep. et m.	Sol in libra.
18	xiv	kl.		
19	xiii	kl.		
20	xii	kl.	Equinoctium.	
21	xi	kl.	S. Mathee apostoli et ev. (r).	Dies.
22	x	kl.	S. Mauricii cum sociis suis.	
23	ix	kl.		
24	viii	kl.		
25	vii	kl.		
26	vi	kl.		
27	v	kl.	SS. Cosme et Damiani mm.	
28	iv	kl.		
29	iii	kl.	S. Michaelis archangeli (b).	
30	ii	kl.	S. Ieronimi presbiteri.	

Hic habet dies paulo minus quam .xii. horas,
Nox autem paulo plus quam .xii.

Additions
5 Dies caniculares finiunt.

Octobris ternum fuge uicenumque secundum.
Sub libra manet hic et scorpius optinet illum.
October habet dies .xxxi. luna .xxix. (sic).

1	KL.		Octobris. S. Remigii ep.
2	vi	Non.	S. Leodegarii ep. et m.
3	v	Non.	
4	iv	Non.	
5	iii	Non.	
6	ii	Non.	S. Fidis v.
7	Non.		S. Marci pape; et Marcelli et Apulei.
8	viii	Id.	
9	vii	Id.	S. DIONISII SOCIORUMQUE eius (r).
10	vi	Id.	S. Paulini ep.
11	v	Id.	
12	iv	Id.	S. Wilfridi ep.
13	iii	Id.	
14	ii	Id.	S. Calixti [pape].
15	Idus		
16	xvii	kl.	Novembris. Octaue S. Dionisii cum sociis.
17	xvi	kl.	S. Aetheldrithe v. Translatio.
18	xv	kl.	S. LVCE EVANGELISTE (b); et Justi m.
19	xiv	kl.	Sol in scorpione.
20	xiii	kl.	Translatio undecim milium virginum (gr).
21	xii	kl.	S. Hilarionis monachi.
22	xi	kl.	Dies.
23	x	kl.	S. Romani ep.
24	ix	kl.	
25	viii	kl.	SS. Crispini et Crispiniani mm.
26	vii	kl.	
27	vi	kl.	VIGILIA.
28	v	kl.	SS. APOSTOLORVM SYMONIS ET IVDE (b).
29	iv	kl.	
30	iii	kl.	Ordinatio S. Swithuni ep. (r).
31	ii	kl.	S. Quintini m. VIGILIA.

Hic habet dies . . . .x. horas,
Nox uero . . . .xiiii.

118

Quinta nouembris obest, ternam de fine cauete.
Scorpius hanc pungit, latet illa sub architenente.
Nouember habet dies .xxx. luna .xxx.

1	KL.		Novembris.	FESTIVITAS OMNIVM Sanctorum (b, r, gr).
2	iv	Non.	S. Eustachii cum sociis suis.	
3	iii	Non.	Hic primat .i. embolismus.	
4	ii	Non.	S. Brinstani ep.	
5	Non.		Dies.	
6	viii	Id.	S. Leonardi conf; et Melanii ep.	
7	vii	Id.		
8	vi	Id.	SS. Quattuor Coronatorum.	
9	v	Id.	S. Theodori m.	
10	iv	Id.		
11	iii	Id.	S. MARTINI EP. (gr); et Menne m.	
12	ii	Id.		
13	Idus		S. Brictii ep.	
14	xviii	kl.	Decembris.	
15	xvii	kl.	S. Machuti ep.	
16	xvi	kl.		
17	xv	kl.	S. Aniani ep.	Sol in sagittario.
18	xiv	kl.	S. Martini Octaue.	
19	xiii	kl.		
20	xii	kl.	S. Eadmundi reg. et m.	
21	xi	kl.		
22	x	kl.	S. CECILIE V.	
23	ix	kl.	S. CLEMENTIS M.; et Felicitatis.	
24	viii	kl.	S. Crisogoni m.	
25	vii	kl.	S. KATERINE V.	
26	vi	kl.	S. Lini [pape].	Primus adventus domini.
27	v	kl.		
28	iv	kl.	Dies.	
29	iii	kl.	S. Saturnini m.	VIGILIA.
30	ii	kl.	S. ANDREE APOSTOLI (gr, b).	

Hic habet dies paulo minus quam .viii. horas,
Nox autem paulo plus quam .xvi.

Dat duodena necem nocet et quindena decembris.
Vtraque letiferum uulnus timet architenentis.
December habet dies .xxxi. luna .xxix.

1	KL.		Decembris.	SS. Crisanti et Darie mm.		
2	iv	Non.		Hic finit .i. embolismus.		
3	iii	Non.	S. Birini ep.	Vltimus adventus dies.		
4	ii	Non.				
5	Non.					
6	viii	Id.	S. NICHOLAI EP. (gr).			
7	vii	Id.	S. Ambrosii ep., et Octaue S. Andree.		Dies.	
8	vi	Id.	CONCEPTIO S. MARIE (b).			
9	v	Id.				
10	iv	Id.				
11	iii	Id.	S. Damasi [pape].			
12	ii	Id.				
13	Idus		S. Judoci conf.; et Lucie v.			
14	xix	kl.	Ianuarii.			
15	xviii	kl.				
16	xvii	kl.	S. Barbare v. et m.	O sapientia (b).		
17	xvi	kl.				
18	xv	kl.	Sol in capricornu.			
19	xiv	kl.				
20	xiii	kl.	VIGILIA.			
21	xii	kl.	S. Thome apostoli.	Solstitium yemale.		
22	xi	kl.	Dies.			
23	x	kl.				
24	ix	kl.				
25	viii	kl.	NATIUITAS DOMINI (b, gr, r). S. Anastasie v.			
26	vii	kl.	S. Stephani prothomartyris (r).			
27	vi	kl.	S. Iohannis euuangeliste (gr).			
28	v	kl.	SS. Innocentium (r).			
29	iv	kl.				
30	iii	kl.				
31	ii	kl.	S. SILVESTRI [PAPE].			

Hic habet dies paulo plus quam .vi. horas,
Nox uero paulo minus quam .xviii.

substantie: sed unitate persone.
am sicut anima rationalis & caro
unus est homo: ita deus & homo
unus est xpistus.
ui passus est p salute nostra: descen
dit ad inferos tercia die resurrexit
a mortuis.
scendit ad celos sedet ad dexteram
dei patris omnipotentis: inde uen
turus iudicare uiuos & mortuos.
Ad cuius aduentum omnes homines
resurgere habent cum corporibz suis:
& reddituri sunt de factis propriis
rationem.
t qui bona egerunt ibunt in uitam
eternam: qui uero mala in ignem
eternum.
ec est fides catholica: quam nisi
quisq; fideliter firmiterq; credide
rit: saluus esse non poterit.

Kyrieleyson. ꝑe eleyson.
ꝑe audi nos. ater de ce
lis deus miserere nobis. Fili redemp
tor mundi deus miserere nobis.
piritus sancte deus miserere nobis.
Sancta trinitas un ds: miserere nobis.
Sancta MARIA ora pro nobis.
Sancta Dei genitrix ora pro nobis.
Sancta Virgo uirginu ora pnobis.
ancte Michael ora pro nobis.
ancte Gabriel ora pro nobis
Sancte Raphael ora pro nobis.
mis sci angli & archangli orate pnob.
omnes sci beatorum spiuum ordines or.
ancte Iohannes baptista ora pnob.
Omis sci Patarche & pphe orate pnob.
Sancte Petre ora pro nobis.
Sancte Paule ora pro nobis
ancte Andrea ora pro nobis.

de substance: mais par le unitet d la psone.
ar si cume la anime rationel e la carn
uns est huem: issi ds e hom uns. e crist.
il ki suffert est pur nre salut: descen
dit a enfers al terz se dreca
de mort.
untat as cels set a la destre deu sun
pere trestut poant: d iloc est auenir
iugier e les uis e les morz.
l aduenement del quel tuz humes
escdrecerunt od lur cors e rendrunt
de lur propres
faiz raisun.
el ki bien furent irunt en la pardu
rable uie: li quel
ueirement mal en pardurable fou.
cest est la commune fei la quele si
chescun fedelement e fermement
crerrat: salf estre
ne porrat.

ancte Iohannes ora pro nobis.
ancte Iacobe. ora pro nobis.
ancte Philippe ora pro nobis.
Sancte Bartholomee ora pnobis.
ancte Ioachee ora pro nob.
Sancte Thoma. ora pro nob.
ancte Iacobe. ora pro nob.
Sancte Symon. ora pro nob.
ancte Taddee. ora pro nob.
Sancte Mathia. ora pro nob.
ancte Barnaba. ora pro nob.
Sancte Luca. ora pnobis
ancte Marce. ora pro nob.
Omis sci apli & euuangeliste. ora pnob
Omis sci discipli dni orate pro nobis.
Omis sci innocentes. orate pro nobis
ancte Stephane. ora pnob.
Sancte Line. ora pnob.
ancte Clete. ora pnob.

Sancte Clemens.	ora pro nobis.
Sancte Syxte.	ora pro nobis.
Sancte Laurenti.	ora pro nobis.
Sancte Corneli.	ora pro nobis.
Sancte Cypriane.	ora pro nobis.
Sancte Vincenti.	ora pro nobis.
Sancte Sebastiane.	ora pro nobis.
Sancte Georgi.	ora pro nobis.
Sancte Victor.	ora pro nobis.
Sancte Dionisii cū sociis tuis orate p
Sancte Maurici cū soc tuis orate pnob.
Sancte ypolite cum sociis tuis orat
Sancte Geruasi & pthasi orate pnob.
Sancte Xpophore.	ora pro nobis.
Sancte Blasi.	ora pro nobis.
Sancte Albane.	ora pro nobis.
Sancte Osuualde.	ora pro nobis.
Sancte Eadmunde.	ora pro nobis.
oms sci martyres.	orate pro nobis.
Sancte Siluester.	ora pro nobis
Sancte Hilari.	ora pro nobis.
Sancte Martine.	ora pro nobis.
Sancte Nicholae.	ora pro nobis.
Sce Ambrosi.	ora pro nobis.
Sancte Augustine.	ora pro nobis.
Sancte Gregori.	ora pro nobis.
Sancte Ieronime.	ora pro nobis.
Sancte Taurine.	ora pro nobis.
Sancte Audoene.	ora pro nobis
Sancte Iohannes.	ora pro nobis
Sancte Augustine cū sociis tuis or
Sancte Cuthberte.	ora pro nobis.
Sancte Ceadda.	ora pro nobis
Sancte Aldelme.	ora pro nobis
Sancte Dunstane.	ora pro nobis.
Sancte Birine.	ra pro nobis
Sancte Swithune.	ra pro nobis.
Sancte Adeluuolde.	ra pro nobis.
Sancte Benedicte.	ra pro nobis
Sancte Maure.	ra pro nobis.

Sancte Philiberte.	ora p nobis
Sancte Columbane.	ora p nobis
Sancte Bertine.	ora pronob
Sancte Egidi.	ora p nobis
Sancte Leonarde.	ora p nobis
Sancte Vuandregisile	ora p nobis
Oms sci confessores	orate pro nobis
sca Maria magdalene.	ora p nobis
Sancta Maria egyptiacha	ora p nobis
Sancta Felicitas.	ora pro nob
Sancta Perpetua.	ora pro nob
Sancta Petronilla.	ora pro nob.
Sancta Agatha.	ora p nobis
Sancta Agnes.	ora pro nob
Sancta Cecilia.	ora pro nob.
Sancta Lucia.	ora pro nob
Sancta Susanna.	ora pro nob.
Sancta Tecla.	ora pro nob.
Sancta oildricha.	ora pronob
Sancta Etheldricha.	ora pro nob
Sancta Ethelburga.	ora pro nob
Sancta hildentha.	ora pro nob
Sancta Vulfilda.	ora pro nob.
Sancta Scolastica.	ora pro nob
Sancta Radegundis.	ora pronob
Sancta Vuareburgis.	ora pro nob.
Sancta Florentia.	ora pro nob.
Sancta Daria.	ora pro nob.
Sancta Columba.	ora pro nob
Sancta Fides.	ora pro nob.
Sancta Spes.	ora pro nob.
Sancta Karitas.	ora pro nob
Sancta Katerina.	ora pro nob.
Sancta Margareta.	ora pro nob.
Sancta Baltildis.	ora pro nob.
Sancta Brigida.	ora pro nob.
Sancta Fidis.	ora pro nob
Sancta Consortia.	ora pro nob.
Omnes sce uirgines	orate pro nob
Omnes sancti.	orate p nob.

The Litany

The Litany which is found on folios 132 recto to 132 verso has the following saints besides the normal run of Apostles:

Martyrs: Stephen, Linus, Cletus, Clement, Sixtus, Lawrence, Cornelius, Cyprian, Vincent, Sebastian, George, Victor, Denis and his companions, Maurice and his companions, Hippolytus and his companions, Gervasius and Protasius, Christopher, Blasius, Alban, Oswald, Edmund.

Confessors: Silvester, Hilary, Martin, Nicolas, Ambrose, Augustine, Gregory, Jerome, Taurinus, Audoenus, John, Augustine and his companions, Cuthbert, Chad, Aldhelm, Dunstan, Birinus, Swithun, **Aethelwold**, Benedict, Maurus, Philibert, Columbanus, Bertin, Leonard, Wandregisil.

Virgins: Mary Magdalene, Mary of Egypt, Felicity, Perpetua, Petronilla, Agatha, Agnes, Cecilia, Lucy, Susanna, Tecla, Mildred, Etheldreda, Ethelburga, Hildelitha, Wulfhilda, Scolastica, Radegund, Walburgis, Florentia, Daria, Columba, Fides, Spes, Karitas, Katherine, Margaret, Baltildis, Bridget, Fides, Consortia.

Though the saints in this litany include some Winchester names such as Birinus, Swithun and **Aethelwold** among the confessors, the general run of the series does not agree with either the litanies of Winchester Cathedral (St Swithun's) as represented by British Museum Cotton MS Vitellius A.XVIII and Oxford Bodleian MS Auct. D.2.6., or with that of Hyde Abbey as found in Oxford Bodleian MS Gough liturg. 8.[30] At St Swithun's are found besides the three saints already mentioned SS Hedda, Frithstan, Birnstan and Alphege 1 among the confessors. At Hyde the sequence is also different, with a double invocation of St Valentine among the martyrs and Judoc and Grimbald among the confessors. SS Edburga and Ethelfleda of Romsey appear among the virgins. All of these Winchester characteristics are missing from Nero C. IV. There is one group of rather unusual English saints among the virgins. These are the three: Ethelburga, Hildelitha and Wulfhilda who were the main saints of the great nunnery of Barking near London. The main part of the litany may be compared with litanies connected with the abbey of Abingdon.[31]

In Nero C. IV there is a group among the Virgins which is not found in the two Abingdon litanies. It consists of: Scolastica, Radegund, Walburgis (Wareburgis), Florentia, Daria, Columba, Fides, Spes, Karitas. With Walburgis for Wareburgis the same group occurs in the Cluniac litany of St Pancras Priory of Lewes.

What we appear to have here is a litany which for the most part resembles that used at Abingdon modified by two groups in the virgins, the first connected with Barking and the second with apparently a Cluniac complexion. Historically there would be nothing unusual in this. The history of the Winchester monasteries is very much bound up with Abingdon, particularly in its great tenth-century period. It is quite possible for the Abingdon pattern of litany to have survived there. The Cluniac modifications can be equally explained by the connection of Henry de Blois with Cluny. The presence of the ladies of Barking cannot be explained. If it had been the Nunnaminster saints it would have been more explicable, but they are absent.

132. The Flagellation. Detail of folio 21

History of the Manuscript

It is unfortunate but we have no definite information about the original owner-ship of Nero C.IV. What is known must be inferred from bits of evidence provided by some entries in the calendar, the litany and one of the prayers. The Winchester element is strong in all three. Besides this Winchester element there is also one which suggests Cluny. We are therefore dealing with an owner connected with Winchester and Cluny. The prayer to St Swithun suggests that he might be the bishop since he says; 'You (St Swithun) are with Christ in the company of saints and I a miserable and weak sinner have sinned in your courts by living ill in your house.' By far the most likely candidate as the original owner is Henry de Blois, bishop of Winchester from 1129 to 1171.[32] He was the brother of King Stephen and one of the most powerful prelates of his day. He had once been a monk of Cluny and held the great abbey of Glastonbury in plurality with the see of Winchester. He is known to have been a collector and lover of works of art and he made splendid gifts to both Glastonbury and Winchester.[33] His dates fit extremely well with that of the Psalter. It would be highly probable that Henry would order a great Psalter for his personal use.

By the middle of the thirteenth century it is certain that the manuscript had migrated to Shaftesbury Abbey, the great nunnery in Dorset, where a number of additions were made to the calendar. These additions cannot be earlier than 1257 when Stephen Bauceyn, the soldier of Henry III was killed by the Welsh. His obit is written in the same hand as the rest of the Shaftesbury additions. It is possible that they were entered at the order of the abbess Juliana Bauceyn who died in 1279.

Under what circumstances the manuscript left Shaftesbury we shall probably never know, nor how it was acquired for the Cottonian collection. It was damaged in the fire of 1731 but not so severely that it has lost any of its beauty or interest.

Notes to the Text

1 H. Omont: *Miniatures Grecs de la Bibliothèque Nationale*, Paris, 1929, pl. XXIV.

2 cf. Omont, *op. cit.* pl. XXXVII.

3 I Samuel 17.38, 39.

4 I Samuel 17.54.

5 I Samuel 17.35.

6 I Samuel 16.13.

7 See F. Wormald: An English Eleventh Century Psalter with Pictures, *Walpole Society*, vol. 38, pls. 4–7.

8 For the iconography of the scenes with Goliath see K. Weitzmann: Prologomena to a Study of the Cyprus Plates, *Metropolitan Museum Journal*, 3 (1970), pp. 97–111.

9 For Pembroke MS 120 see E. Parker: A Twelfth-Century Cycle of New Testament Drawings from Bury St Edmunds Abbey, *Proceedings of the Suffolk Institute of Archaeology*, XXXI, part 3 (1969), pp. 263–302; for the leaves in the British Museum, the Victoria and Albert Museum and the Pierpont Morgan Library, see M. R. James: Four Leaves of an English Psalter, *Walpole Society*, vol. 25 (1937), pp. 1–23.

10 British Museum Lansdowne MS 383, folio 12 verso, see E. G. Millar: *English Illuminated Manuscripts from the Xth to the XIIIth Century*, Paris and Brussels, 1926, pl. 33a.

11 British Museum. Cotton MS Galba A. XVIII, folios 2 verso, 21.

12 See F. Wormald: *The Antiquaries Journal*, XLVII (1967), 159–165 where the painting is reproduced.

13 See British Museum. Add. MS 24199, folio 18 reproduced by F. Wormald: *English Drawings of the Tenth and Eleventh Century*, London, 1952, p. 28, pl. 6a.

14 W. Koehler: *Dumbarton Oaks Papers*, I, 1940, pp. 63–87.

15 Oxford, Bodl. MS Lat. liturg. 5 (S.C. 29744), see J. J. G. Alexander: *Anglo-Saxon Illumination in Oxford Libraries*, Oxford, 1970, pls. 26–29.

16 New York, Pierpont Morgan Library, MS 708, see B. da Costa Greene and M. Harrsen: *The Pierpont Morgan Library, Exhibition of Illuminated Manuscripts held at the New York Public Library*, New York, 1934, pl. 19.

17 folio 43 verso, see C. R. Dodwell: *The Canterbury School of Illumination 1066–1200*, Cambridge, 1954, pl. 26c.

18 See C. M. Kauffmann: The Bury Bible, *Journal of the Warburg and Courtauld Institutes*, XXIX (1966). pp. 60–81.

19 See T. S. R. Boase: *English Art 1100–1216*, Oxford, 1953, pl. 50a.

20 Oxford, Bodl. MS Auct. D.2.6. (S.C. 3636), folio 156 ff., see O. Pächt: The Illustrations of St. Anselm's Prayers and Meditations, *Journal of the Warburg and Courtauld Institutes*, XIX (1956), pp. 68–83.

21 Le Mans Bibliothèque Municipale, MS 263, see Bibliothèque Nationale, *Les Manuscrits à Peintures en France du VIIe au XIIe Siècle*, Paris, 1954, no. 321.

22 See Yves Bonnefoy: *Peinture Murales de la France Gothique*, Paris, 1954, p. 8, pls. 1–5.

23 cf. Otto Demus: *The Mosaics of Norman Sicily*, London, 1950, pls. 3, 63.

24 See G. and M. Sotiriou: *Icones du Mont Sinaï*, Athens, 1956, figs. 78, 92; also Kurt Weitzmann: *Studies in Classical and Byzantine Manuscript Illumination*, Chicago, 1971, particularly pp. 271–313.

25 K. Weitzmann: Icon Painting in the Crusader Kingdom, *Dumbarton Oaks Papers*, XX (1966), pp. 52, 53, pl. I. The icon shows Christ enthroned.

26 See F. Wormald: An English Eleventh Century Psalter with Pictures, *Walpole Society*, vol. 38, pl. 8.

27 O. Pächt, C. R. Dodwell, F. Wormald: *The St. Albans Psalter*, London, 1960, p. 206, pl. 41.

28 See C. M. Kauffmann. The Bury Bible, *Journal of the Warburg and Courtauld Institutes*, XXIX (1966), pl. 25d.

29 Particularly folio 456 recto.

30 Printed by J. B. L. Tolhurst, *The Monastic Breviary of Hyde Abbey, Winchester*, V (Henry Bradshaw Soc. LXXI), F.G. 66–67 verso.

31 They are the printed Breviary of Abingdon in Emmanuel College, Cambridge and a Psalter in the Cambridge University Library, MS Dd. i. 20.

32 John le Neve: *Fasti Ecclesiae Anglicanae 1066–1300*, II (Monastic Cathedrals), ed. Diana E. Greenway, London, 1971, p. 85.

33 See E. Bishop: *Liturgica Historica*, Oxford, 1918, pp. 392–401, and David Knowles: *The Monastic Order in England*, Cambridge, 1941, pp. 280–293.

List of Illustrations

133. Jacob wrestling with the Angel. Detail of folio 5